# Advance Praise for *Gaiamancy* . . .

"In *Gaiamancy* Maureen Belle has called upon the wisdom of her ancestors, her background as a renowned environmental designer, and her deep understanding of the invisible but powerful flow of energy within the earth to present a valuable and usable guide to bringing balance and harmony into our living environments."

—Denise Linn
Author of *Sacred Space* and *The Secret Language of Signs*

To Virginia

Blessings, Maureen

# GAIAMANCY

# GAIAMANCY
## Creating Harmonious Environments

MAUREEN L. BELLE

WHITE DOE PRODUCTIONS
GREENBANK, WASHINGTON

Published by: **White Doe Productions**
               **PO Box AB**
               **Greenbank, WA 98253**

Edited by Elana Freeland and Ellen Kleiner
Book design and typography by Richard Harris
Cover production by Janice St. Marie

A Blessingway book

Printed in the United States of America on acid-free recycled paper

**Publisher's Cataloging-in-Publication**
Belle, Maureen L.
      Gaiamancy : creating harmonious environments / Maureen L.
   Belle. — 1st ed.
     p. cm.
     Includes bibliographical references and index.
     Preassigned LCCN: 98-60095
     ISBN: 0-9662622-0-4

    1. Geomancy.  2. Feng-shui.  3. Interior architecture.  4. Environmental
design.  5. Medicine wheels.  6. Wheels—Religious aspects.   I. Title

  BF1779.F4B45 1998                           133.3'33
                                           QB198-369

10  9  8  7  6  5  4  3  2  1

*With special thanks to:*

Elana, for the fine-tuning and gift of storytelling she brought to the editing;
Ellen, for diving in and bringing the book to its elegant completion, and
  for all the late-night support when I thought I couldn't go any further;
Shaun Edward, for such a wonderful spirit and inspiration;
Denise Linn, for her friendship, faith, support, and mentorship, as well
  as her uncompromising integrity;
Sister Christine, "Cecil," for her loving support and guidance;
Ingrid, for all her help and support;
All family members and friends who saw me through the birthing of this
  book.

Thanks also to Trish, for that book on feng shui;
to the teachers, both in body and beyond, who so lovingly passed on
  their truths and helped me awaken to my own;
and to all writers, shamans, and medicine people, ancient and contemporary, who passed on the knowledge needed to bring Gaiamancy
  to life.
All other contributors to this pathway, know that you are honored and
  are written here in Spirit.

This book is dedicated to
"La Dottie"—
for her unfailing faith in me
and for the spirit of adventure she passed on
in her inimitable style

# Contents

# List of Figures

## Chapter 5

## Chapter 7

## Chapter 10

# Introduction

*When you follow your bliss, and by bliss I mean the deep sense of being in it and doing what the push is out of your own existence—you follow that, and doors will open where you would not have thought there would be doors. And where there wouldn't be a door for anyone else.*

—Joseph Campbell

As an environmental consultant, I offer relatively toxin-free materials and finishes to clients who are building or remodeling. My goal is to ensure that their living and working environments are as safe as I know how to make them. But "safe" buildings are not good enough. Without grace, harmony, and balance, even the most nontoxic settings will be defective—a fact of life I learned from the inside out.

I began working in my father's builder-developer business when I was twelve years old. There I came to know the parameters of beams, concrete block walls, and wooden framing, and I became instinctively aware of the inner cores of buildings. In fact, I was intimately familiar with residential, commercial, and industrial construction before I could calculate an algebraic equation. By age twenty, I had helped design a housing tract, specifying materials and creating "sub" timelines. I then began building homes by hand and remodeling buildings for my own business! Before long, I realized I had the knowledge needed to tackle all sorts of construction projects, but I hadn't yet discovered how much I *didn't* know.

1

At age twenty-nine, I decided to build a house from the ground up. I hired a carpenter, and together we started the laborious process of clearing a site and creating the structure—an approach I recommend to architects, engineers, and designers alike. At the time, I was raising a son alone, operating a gallery/yarn and gift shop out of an old house I had remodeled, and holding weaving and spinning classes at night. Hey, I figured, what's one more project when you're in your twenties?

To seal the exposed beams in the interior of the house, we used a highly toxic product, currently outlawed in the United States, along with what I now know are extremely toxic standard building materials, adhesives, and finishes. I trusted the products of manufacturers who appeared to have my best interests at heart. The exposure, however, was too much for my immune system; I contracted chemical pneumonia and soon slipped into chronic fatigue. Only later did I realize how compromised my immune system had already been. Dedication to being "a good worker" had almost become an epitaph on my tombstone!

Soon after the chronic fatigue set in, my options became clear: either I choose a spiritual path or I die. Of course, I still believed in a productive life and in work as an expression of creativity, but not to the point of losing my physical, emotional, and mental well-being. Nevertheless, I eventually had to close down my successful business, for I had come to the brink of death more than once. The good news is that this illness catapulted me toward a turning point in my life and my career.

With a sick body, I learned how to be strong and spiritually centered. A longtime student of yoga, I continued to practice this discipline. I also took up the martial art of Tae Kwon Do with a Vietnamese master, as well as Tai Chi and dance—all of which awakened physical forces to draw upon. Feeling the forces of *ch'i* moving through my body, I then sought to amplify their effects.

I remembered to listen and observe everything around me. I heard the voice of the wind spirit; colors became almost blindingly brilliant; I even saw people's souls shining around their bodies. In effect, I'd returned to the wisdom I had as a child, when I talked to animals, trees, rocks, and faeries. Soon those early conversations themselves came flooding back to me, whereupon I began talking to everything in my midst. I discovered that my imaginary friends from childhood were *real,* as was the guardian angel who used to sit on my bed and comfort me, telling me everything was going to be OK. And in my meditations I found a deep, abiding love from Spirit.

In addition to these practices, I also drew strength from earlier years of wildcrafting and tending animals on a ranch. While in the woods gathering dye plants for yarn and medicinal plants for curing ailments, I had learned to listen to plant spirits. My nonhuman neighbors soon became as familiar to me as family and friends. I could *feel* trees as they shared their willingness to provide shelter and warmth with their "bones," and *hear* how glad they were to do this for us, provided that we did not overstep their offering.

So it was that my near-death turning point opened up new worlds to me. I was discovering another way of being—and with it, a new way of perceiving. I realized that we walk on the bones of ancestors and share the planet with many gentle friends in the realms of nature who gift us daily. I saw, too, that our job is simply to nurture, foster, and learn from these entities, then pass on. In the course of fulfilling these job requirements, we lose the sense of ownership and move into partnership with our businesses, homes, and tracts of land, becoming their guardians rather than their possessors.

It was during my years of recovery and concomitant university training that environmental harmony and balance became at least as important to me as environmental safety. It was also at this time that Gaiamancy (GUY-uh-man-see) began to take shape in my mind as a life-supportive approach to site layout and building design. Derived from the word *Gaia,* meaning "spirit and body of the living earth," and the suffix *-mancy,* defined as "deriving knowledge from," the term *Gaiamancy* means "deriving knowledge from the spirit and body of the living earth." When asked how this notion differs from that of geomancy, I would reply that Gaiamancy, rooted in *Gaia,* views the earth as a sentient being with a soul, whereas the prefix *geo-* refers to the earth as a composite of elements, as it is commonly thought of in works on geology or geometry.

Not only does Gaiamancy draw from the sacred earth sciences, but it assists in eliminating centuries of semantic confusion. It also encompasses a *variety* of divinatory practices rooted in the disciplines with which I am most familiar, such as feng shui, the Chinese art of placement; Native American, Celtic, and Hawaiian applications; and *vastu shastra,* the Vedic system of sacred architecture. Included in this hologram is a modern-day approach to environmental safety.

The evolution of Gaiamancy is intriguing. It was seeded by my early childhood experiences with Celtic and Native American teachers. It then sprang into being following my studies of the more than 5,000-year-old Chinese Taoist art of feng shui, which addresses the movement of energy in the natural world. In my work with architectural design, feng shui principles came to be represented by the Chinese *bagua,* a form of divination based on our interconnectedness with all things animate and inanimate. Modern-day quantum physicists depict this interrelationship via the spaces between "quarks," which form the source of life. So it is that contemporary Western physics, like ancient Eastern Taoism, recognizes that out of the pregnant "void" issues forth the fabric of life, that there is an ongoing dance of interdependence between matter and spirit, and that we are all a part of one another and of everything around us.

Over time, Gaiamancy expanded to encompass the Celtic and Native American perspectives from my heritage. These influences were integrated into the practice of Gaiamancy for two reasons. First, because some of my clients could not identify with the Chinese *bagua,* and I wanted to develop models that would work for them. In addition, deriving knowledge from these forms enlivened my connection with my ancestors.

I felt an immediate affinity with Celtic ways because my mother's family was mostly Irish. Growing up, I was nurtured by my maternal grandmother's stories of her parents' journey from Ireland to Montana. Once settled, they brought over other family members, providing food, clothing, and a room for them in their large home until the new arrivals could find work and move out on their own. I heard numerous accounts of suffering as a result of the potato famine and of grieving over the loss of their beloved land. There must have been a Druid or two in my lineage, considering how "fey" I've been since childhood.

My father's people were a mixed lot. His mother, of Spanish and Apache-Cherokee descent, was a *curandera,* a skilled healer who knew well the medicinal power of herbs. She lost her father at an early age, and to help support her family she relied on her knowledge of herbal remedies. My father's father was from Turino, in northern Italy. He left home as a teenager to explore the world, defying the familial immersion in engineering and mechanics. Soon after arriving in the southwestern United States, he met my grandmother. My gift from this beloved explorer may have been a high degree of wanderlust infused with a love of adventure.

Indeed, as soon as my health began to improve, I set forth on a quest of my own. I attended architecture classes in Rome—as part of a five-year professional degree I was completing in interior architecture through the University of Oregon School of Architecture—and spent time in England, Belgium, Austria, Switzerland, France, Germany, Greece, Yugoslavia, and Hawaii. I traveled to Central America, South America, and the Bahamas to research whale and dolphin interspecies communication. Everywhere I went I was drawn to the indigenous people, eager to learn of their time-honored earth wisdom and to integrate it into my practice of Gaiamancy. While walking their lands, I came to honor the ancient ones who devised the sacred forms and held them in safekeeping for our times.

The more I traveled, the more convinced I was that the earth is not only a sphere made up of mineral, vegetable, and animal elements, but a living, breathing being! No matter what continent I was on, I heard whispers of an old story: Long ago, when we humans came to this planet, we promised Gaia, together with her rock and mineral people, her green people, her four-leggeds, and all others, that we would not harm them, that we would respect and love and learn from them. Gaiamancy was therefore conceived not only as a path of healing, balance, and harmony but also as a way of *remembering our promise.*

Remembering this vow, made thousands of years ago—long before humanity slipped into its deep sleep—is simply a matter of going into the earth, into Gaia. Knowledge of our connectedness with her, although forgotten, is not lost and does not require the divination of a high priest or priestess. As I tell my clients, "I am here to enhance your intent. I mediate; *you* interact with your environment." Nor is it necessary to invent a course of study to access earth wisdom. At great sacrifice, blessed elders have held such knowledge for us, to be released when the time is right; and according to the old story I heard whispered round the world, *the time is now right.* We can at last learn once-sacred secrets from others. Having done so, we can add our own unique insights and pass on the gift, extending around the planet a ribbon of light connecting one person with another, and yet another.

Most people on this continent of Turtle Island, as North America is called in many sacred traditions, have a rich and varied lineage; we are the "rainbow people." As such, we are able to draw from wisdom that spans the continents, which is precisely what this book strives to do, all the while presenting the knowledge in simplified form to keep its sacredness intact. To do less would be to dishonor those who have held it for us over the millennia.

The purpose of *Gaiamancy* is threefold: to show you how I work with the principles of traditional earth wisdom, to help you apply them to your home or work space, and to invite you to add to this cumulative body of living knowledge by reaching into the earth-inspired memories that pulse through your own being. To make the most of this guidebook, relate the interpretations of energy flow to your own habitat, apply the solutions most appealing to you, and incorporate into your everyday life the eight "practices" interspersed throughout the chapters. For further assistance, a pronunciation guide, glossary of terms, and listing of selected books and other resource guides, products, schools, seminars, and training institutes are included at the end of the book.

You are participating in a glorious dance with Gaia. So slip on your dancing shoes and prepare to trip the light fantastic while reshaping your surroundings to harmonize with the living, loving world around you!

Part One

# The Energetics of Gaiamancy

## Chapter One

# The Quest for Sacred Space

*Our deepest fear is not that we are inadequate. Our deepest fear is that we are powerful beyond measure. It is our light, not our darkness, that most frightens us. We ask ourselves, who am I to be brilliant, gorgeous, talented, fabulous? Actually, who are you not to be? You are a child of God. Your playing small does not serve the world. . . . As we let our own light shine, we unconsciously give other people permission to do the same. As we are liberated from our own fear, our presence automatically liberates others.*

—His Holiness the Dalai Lama

W e are beautiful and powerful beings who have a supportive, loving friend just beneath our feet. To return to the center of our lives, we must recognize the sacredness of the ground we walk upon. With this return will come harmony, balance, and vitality.

Division between earth and spirit does not exist; they are one and the same. Our perception of this separation is an illusion, an illness. We of Western cultures tend to believe that to be in spiritual harmony we must leave the earth, either physically or through prayer or meditation. What grief we have caused our earth by clinging to this ideology! In our state of always wanting and never having, and of living in subsequent fear and disappointment, we have set the stage for vast destruction of the planet through greed and domination. What is of spirit is of earth, and what is of earth is of spirit. It is *humankind's actions* that are often not of spirit.

The message that Gaia is alive and not doing well is conveyed not to elicit guilt, but rather to underscore the fact that we are ultimately united with the earth and one another. The essence of this simple truth comes through grappling with the conflict and change that constitute such a large portion of our lives on this planet. For years, my experience of life was colored by pain, frustration, denial, and separation. Like the Chinese *konji* for a word that means both crisis and opportunity, my situation was anything but "bad karma" or poor luck; instead, it was guiding me toward my birthright of a full, rich way of being. Suddenly, I began to recognize the sacred in my so-called mundane, everyday life. With that, I came to understand the interconnectedness of all—also known as the Tao behind daily living, or the *soyal,* the blending, according to the Hopi who have been holding this sacred knowledge for us for hundreds of years.

Such connectedness we learn from Gaia. In a slide show I often present, I have the audience look at treetops and out into the sky to reenact the customary human search for the sacred. I then remind them that "the heavens" are not the only place where the sacred resides, that it dwells here on earth too—in each and every one of us, human and nonhuman alike, as well as in our interactions. I go on to explain that when we are able to recognize the sanctity of every part of our lives, including our currently unconscious habits, we will be living in this profound state of connectedness.

From brushing our teeth to clothing our bodies, from eating breakfast to reading before we fall asleep at night, our actions will then express our sense of the sacred, for they will be initiated through our *intention.* Habits made conscious through intention become ritual, and ritual has a life of its own, entwining us with the rhythms of the earth.

Recognizing that our "everyday" acts are sacred is therefore a critical step we must take in the quest to balance our lives.

Consider homekeeping, for example. I greatly enjoy "puttering around" the house watering plants, dusting, sorting and cleaning, vacuuming. These small, humble acts, when performed unhurriedly, become a ritual dance that sparks a warm, intimate interaction with the world around me. I call it a "humming" way of being.

Some of my friends think I am crazy for enjoying housework, but they have humming rituals of their own. Holding and rocking an infant is such a ritual, as is gardening, especially digging in the soil while watching, smelling, and listening to the growing plants of the earth. Whether you are cleaning house or planting corn, creating a piece of art, combing your child's hair, walking on the beach, or collecting stones and feathers, the way is the same.

I recall a several-year interlude in which I forgot to allow for puttering. Oh, what a busy, stressful, barren time that was! Then when I finally escaped the "hamster wheel" of productivity, the humming returned.

Many of us are rediscovering "home" on this beautiful planet, and in the process, finding that the *entire planet* is home. For centuries, human beings the world over have been taught that home is "heaven," the "afterlife," where they would be at peace and happy with themselves and others. A more interlinking belief is that we are home here on earth. When we learn to equate home with the macrocosm of the planet and the microcosm of our bodies, a sense of harmony arises with no struggle and surprisingly little effort. At that point we remember we are in spirit and out of ego, in wholeness and out of either-or dichotomies.

Joseph Campbell, the well-known mythologist, once said to his classes at Sarah Lawrence College: If you want to help people, teach them how to live here on the planet, in this world. The ancient Roman philosopher Ovid wrote of a time when all people lived in harmony with one another and with nature. Plato referred to the Age of Cronos, when humans enjoyed abundance in harmony with the spirits of the earth. This part of our heritage, long forgotten, is now being "unearthed."

We are in the process of transforming human consciousness into a state of being that seeks cooperation instead of competition, that celebrates diversity and acknowledges the interconnectedness of all. The old paradigm operated on the basis of separation, boundaries, ownership, you-against-me, us-against-them. The new paradigm is of an altogether different nature, and not just the opposite face of the old; we are learning to be in synchrony with others' rhythms, including those of the planet, for we are now aware that we are children of the earth and that her rhythms are ours as well.

Along with these transformations, we are learning to create environments that reflect the seasonal changes, that are in synchrony with the earth's sacred breath—places that are stimulating and empowering as well as peaceful. In simply understanding that we are continually linking up with our environment on a cellular level, we become enlivened and supported by it, as it is by us. We begin to catch glimpses of the hundreds of subtle interactions that occur moment to moment, a phenomenon that can be experienced while working with practice 1 on page 15. The next step is to ensure that the environments we are creating are balanced enough to provide the support and life-giving energy we need in order not just to survive but to thrive.

*Practice 1*

## Sending Roots into the Earth

To experience the connection you have with Gaia, try sending your awareness into the earth, an exercise I learned from a medicine woman, healer, and dear friend in Northern California. The purpose of this practice is to pass beyond the material structure of the building you are in, and to connect with the portion of the earth that supports it.

~ Sit comfortably in a chair or on a carpeted floor, preferably with your bare feet flat on the floor. Close your eyes and breathe calmly, taking seven full, deep breaths.

~ When you feel relaxed, envision ribbons of light extending from the soles of your feet into the earth below. Imagine the ribbons passing like roots of a tree through the carpet, wood, and concrete; down into the soil; and through rock, water, and fire toward the center of the earth.

~ As the ribbons approach the solid core of the earth, find a place to secure them. Tie them tightly yet lovingly, forming bows if you wish. Then slowly follow the ribbons back up to the surface, taking time to see, feel, hear, taste, and touch the earth as you pass through it. While tracing the ribbons to the outermost layer of the earth, you will be using hundreds of as-yet-undefined senses. Honor them and you will soon feel the warmth and infinite love that Gaia holds for you.

*Chapter Two*

# Using Wheels As Overlays

*It is not because things are difficult that we do not dare; it is because we do not dare that they are difficult.*

—Seneca

E ach of Gaia's modes of self-expression can be presented graphically in the shape of a wheel, or circle. Such information can be arranged in the form of a square, too, but then it would not convey as strong a sense of continuity or integration. Just as the circularity of the wheel is used for charting astrological data and for creating healing mandalas, so too can it be used for representing geomantic influences and for designing sacred living spaces in accordance with them.

When it comes to interpreting the forces affecting an environment, the wheel is a profound device. It immediately demystifies principles that are difficult to articulate, and clarifies interactions that defy logic. Only after years of struggling to devise a language for Gaiamancy did I arrive at this discovery. Soon after adopting the wheel as a format, I was delighted to find that it serves both the linear mind and the penetrating spirit. Aware that feng shui had its own "wheel," known as the *bagua,* I then began constructing a wheel for each of the other sacred practices I had studied.

Drawing any one of these wheels on a sheet of tracing paper, I found I could place it over the blueprint of a lot or building drawn to scale, or of a neighborhood, city, or state. Using the wheel as an overlay, I was able to interpret the movement of energy through all sorts of places. The more I worked with these wheels, the more attuned I became to the relationship between people and their immediate environment, between their environment and its surroundings, and between the many subtle and not-so-subtle energies converging in any particular location. Using intuition and other geomantic tools, I could then recommend practical solutions for enhancing the quality of energy in home and work spaces. In short, the wheels helped me see where force fields were out of balance and how to reestablish harmony within them.

The wheels I most often use today are the Chinese *bagua* wheel, the Native American medicine wheel, and the Celtic wheel, each of which is described below. Sometimes I'll use one of them exclusively, or intermingled with elements of a wheel from the Vedic, Tibetan, or Hawaiian traditions; other times I'll use all three wheels simultaneously. In some respects, the eight-sided *bagua* wheel, eight-spoked medicine wheel, and eight-latticed Celtic wheel are remarkably similar, reminiscent of the ribbons of light that wind around the planet. In other respects, these wheels are strikingly unique. The important point to remember while working with them is that although they are all derived from the spirit of Gaia, respect and purity of heart must be shown to the keepers of each tradition.

## The Three Wheels

Working with these wheels has taught me that each one indeed has a "voice" of its own. As you read the simplified background information below—as well as the more detailed practical applications described in chapters 3, 4, and 5—listen deeply to these voices and decide which one feels most familiar to you.

## The Chinese *Bagua* Wheel

The ribbon of light that inspired the Chinese *bagua* wheel spans 5,000 years of Eastern knowledge. I was introduced to this overlay (see figure 2–1) through my studies of Tibetan Buddhism, the *I Ching,* feng shui, and Qi Gong.

Initially, I learned that the *bagua* form of divination began in Tibet with the shell of a turtle, which was used as an auger, or divining tool, to interpret a slice of time in the cosmos. First the turtle was ceremonially killed, then the shell was cracked and "read." The inner shell was said to reflect the universal yin forces created by heaven, and the outer shell the universal yang forces. In ancient Chinese cosmology these twin aspects of nature were believed to have the following properties:

Figure 2–1 *Chinese bagua wheel overlay*

| Yin | Yang |
|---|---|
| Feminine | Masculine |
| Dark | Light |
| Soft | Hard |
| Absorbing | Deflecting |
| Moon | Sun |
| Negative | Positive |
| Intuitive | Linear |
| Receptive | Assertive |

The turtle, especially the sea turtle, is regarded as a divinatory form in many cultures, perhaps because it bridges two worlds—land and water— and lives a long life, often thriving for more than 100 years. Hawaiians, who greatly revere the turtle, call it *honu,* a term similar to *honua,* Hawaiian for earth. The shell of *honu* provided a grid for stellar navigation during long Polynesian voyages that led to the "discovery" of Hawaii.

Native Americans refer to North America as Turtle Island. Other

Native American teachings describe Earth Mother as a turtle swimming through the cosmos with the earth on her back. It is said that the earth's crust, like the turtle's shell, bears a network of lines showing the magnetic web of energy both surrounding the planet and within it.

Hawaiian, Native American, and Chinese legends alike correlate the thirteen segments on a turtle's back with the thirteen moons of the lunar calendar. (See figure 2–2.)

Figure 2–2 Thirteen moons on turtle's back

According to Chinese lore, in about 3000 BCE Fu Hsi, a mythical being described as part human and part snake, discovered on a sea turtle's back eight trigrams as well as a map of the heavens. Ancient diviners went on to write the *I Ching* (*Book of Changes*) based on these eight trigrams and the resulting sixty-four hexagrams; each of the trigrams consisted of a combination of three lines, broken ones signifying yin and continuous ones signifying yang. The earliest name for the *I Ching* was *Chou I* (*Changes of Chou*), a book compiled by tribal people from the mountains of northwest China as they migrated south around 1325 BCE, bringing their turtle oracle with them. The sixty-four hexagrams of the *I Ching* are still in use today.

Interestingly, in recent years a similarity has been noted between these sixty-four hexagrams and the sixty-four combinations of proteins that make up human DNA, only a small percentage of which are "turned on" to activate our potential. The inference is that since consulting the *I Ching* has been known to increase our sense of harmony, and since DNA's molecular strands have been shown to strengthen under harmonious conditions, this divinatory practice has the capacity to turn on as yet unexpressed aspects of our being!

In my studies I also learned about the three main schools of feng shui—the form school, the compass school, and the Tibetan Black Hat school—all of which rely on the *I Ching*. The form school originated in Kuang-shi, in southwest China, when a ninth-century scholar named Yang Yun-sung recorded a collection of folk practices based on *ch'i,* the universal cosmic energy that moves like wind and water. The compass school emerged in northern China, assigning directions and characteristics to the flow of *ch'i.*

Both the form and compass schools employ astrology and an intricate geomancer's compass known as a *lo pan*—a flat disk divided into several rings, in the center of which is a magnetic needle. The innermost ring bears the eight trigrams of the *I Ching;* the surrounding twenty or so rings contain information about the eight directions, signs of the zodiac, movement of planets, Chinese calendar, and much more. Some *lo pan* have been translated into English and can be purchased through resources listed at the back of this book.

The Tibetan Black Hat approach is more eclectic, combining Tibetan Tantric Buddhism with Tibetan Bon and Chinese folk practices, as well as aspects of Confucianism, Taoism, and traditional feng shui. The Taoist viewpoint embraced by this school has been of special appeal to Westerners. For example, the Black Hat sect places the bottommost trigram of the *bagua* wheel (usually associated with north) at the main door entry to a dwelling rather than aligning it with the magnetic north pole—a sensible custom in our modern world where few lots are laid out in accordance with the compass points. The practice of Gaiamancy is based on this positioning of the *bagua* wheel.

Ultimately, the use of the *bagua* wheel in Gaiamancy was triggered by three synchronous events. While studying interior architecture at the

University of Oregon School of Architecture, I took Qi Gong classes with a Chinese master and was given a book on feng shui. These simultaneous immersions awakened within me a connection between the influence of *ch'i,* or life force, on and in buildings and its effect on and within the human body.

*Ch'i,* often called cosmic breath, is an energy felt but rarely seen. Depending on its flow, it can be either gentle and supportive or ferocious and challenging, if not overwhelming. Pathways that allow for long, linear flows of *ch'i,* for example, can spell catastrophe, as is demonstrated by our straight, narrow streets and waterways. These configurations invite cosmic energy to pass too quickly through them. Just as linear waterways tend to flood the surrounding landscape, linear streets are apt to deplete vital life forces. The art of feng shui (wind and water) was devised to help avert such disasters.

Our ancestors knew that wind and water carry both the power of life and the power of death. What's more, they knew these forces are most likely to be life-enhancing when *ch'i,* the divine breath, produces a gentle ebb and flow of invisible energy. This wisdom of the old ones became apparent to me while visiting ancient cities and observing that early residents most often chose to establish their dwellings in gently breezy places near springs, rivers, lakes, or seas. In part, this decision was driven by such practical considerations as the need for crop irrigation and transportation. Yet the ebb and flow of *invisible* energy no doubt played an important role as well. Indeed, scientists have since proved that moving water produces negative ions—charged atoms that both heal and enervate the body.

## The Native American Medicine Wheel

When I first began working with the Native American medicine wheel, I experienced an instant sense of recognition that inspired me to further explore this conduit to knowledge. Originally, the North American continent was home to over 500 First Nation tribes, some with their own medicine wheel—a stone circle or hoop used for telling time, following the seasons, and conducting spiritual practices. Although the assignment of colors, elements, and animal and plant spirits to parts of the wheel differed from tribe to tribe, each variation contained the same four directions (east, south, west, and north) and often the same four colors (red, white, black, and yellow) to signify the four human races, thus revealing an age-old congruity in belief systems.

The medicine wheel I created for use as an overlay (see figure 2–3) is a composite of hoops walked by several First Nation peoples. Elders have ensured that it has been correctly and respectfully crafted in accordance with ancestral traditions. As you will see in chapter 4, this wheel is multilayered and holographic—and for good reason. In much the same way that *I Ching* hexagrams reflect our DNA, the macrocosmic medicine wheel spirals its travelers into microcosmic DNA (see figure 2–4). Indeed, those who have walked the hoop report that it "holds a remembrance" of their physical existence, each round awakening a long-buried memory, and with it a deep form of "knowing."

The Native American medicine wheel can also trigger an awareness of the sacred geometry of our physical, emotional, mental, and spiritual bodies—revealing the beauty of who we truly are. As such, in walking this wheel of life we are able to find counsel to apply to the layout and design of the buildings we live and work in as well as to our lives as a whole.

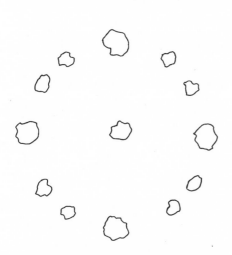

Figure 2–3 Native American
medicine wheel overlay

Figure 2–4 Human DNA spiral

## The Celtic Wheel

I created the Celtic wheel after consulting my ancestors and studying the seasons of the Celts. I was inspired, too, by the first century CE Coligny calendar found in France in 1897, which begins on October 31 with Samhain, the Celtic New Year's Eve, and starts each month at the full moon. Hence, incorporated into this overlay (see figure 2–5) is an honoring of lunar events. Also included are trees and animals, both of which played a significant role in the lives of early Celts.

The Celtic wheel is modeled on one of the oldest forms of Celtic art—namely, the spiral, depicted variously as a single spiral (see figure 2–6), a double spiral (see figure 2–7), or a labyrinth (see figure 2–8). Found throughout Europe in artwork and carvings as well as on clothing and jewelry, the spiral signifies passage to "the center," or a pathway to spirit. Mazes abound in Ireland, and only after walking one did I draft this labyrinthine wheel.

Figure 2–5 Celtic wheel overlay

Other components unique to the Celtic wheel overlay are sacred objects, such as the cauldron (see figure 2–9), ancient Celtic symbol of nourishment, warmth, knowledge, fulfillment, and divination. Cauldrons typically held a treasure such as a pot of gold or a magic potion.

Many people who are unaccustomed to Eastern or Native American perspectives are drawn strongly to the Celtic wheel. In fact, this overlay has proved highly transformational among individuals of European lineage.

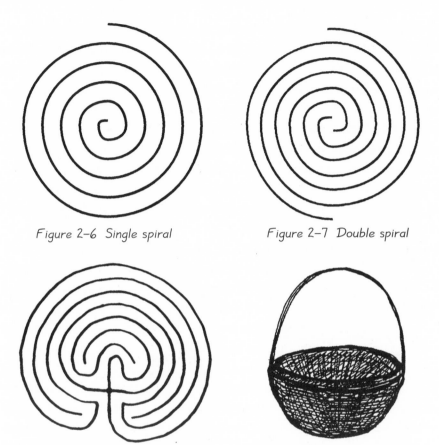

Figure 2–6  Single spiral

Figure 2–7  Double spiral

Figure 2–8  Traditional labyrinth

Figure 2–9  Cauldron

## Working with the Wheels

Knowing the derivation and emphasis of each of the three primary wheels of Gaiamancy, you may have already decided on the one that most resonates with your approach to life. If so, this is most likely the format you will want to use in evaluating and balancing your home or work space. If not, take heart—the following three chapters will help you examine your surroundings in each of these modes, one of which is apt to spark a sense of the familiar.

In each instance, you will find a labeled diagram of the wheel under discussion. Sketch the diagram onto tracing paper, adding the labels provided; you will then have a replica of the wheel to use as an overlay. Next, reduce your plot plan or floor plan to the size of the overlay, and draw a circle or oval through its outermost points. (If you do not know the shape of the lot supporting your home or office, ask the building manager or owner for a photocopy of the blueprint; your city or county can also access these records for you.) Then superimpose the tracing-paper sketch of the wheel over the plan you wish to evaluate.

While working with your overlay, remember that the wheel is malleable. It can be "stretched" to fit the shape of any lot or building, as is illustrated below.

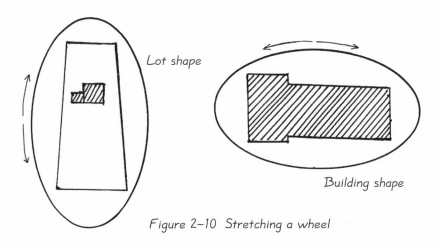

Lot shape

Building shape

Figure 2–10  Stretching a wheel

Remember, too, that your overlay can help you balance smaller spaces, such as a room or the top of your desk. Simply place the overlay over a drawing of the area, lining up the bottom of the wheel with the wall containing the main entry door or with the side of the desk that faces your chair. And never leave home without it; in fact, fold up the overlay and tuck it in your travel kit. Moving a wastebasket or placing special objects in strategic locations can transform a stagnant or chaotic hotel or motel room into a safe, well-balanced sanctuary.

Whether you choose to align your environment with the *bagua* wheel, medicine wheel, Celtic wheel, or all three, it will have a profound effect. For very soon you will be living the sacred life and it will be living you!

Now let us walk each wheel in turn . . .

*Chapter Three*

# The Chinese Bagua Wheel

*A good traveler has no fixed plans and is not intent on arriving.*
—Lao-tzu (570–490 BCE)

The *bagua* wheel is built upon the eight trigrams of the *I Ching*. It also contains the ancient Chinese groupings of elements, colors, directions, and facets of life associated with these phenomena.

## Special Characteristics

The elements—in addition to the earth, air, fire, and water believed by Westerners to comprise the physical universe—include metal and wood. Metal, in ancient China, was seen as the coming together of old and new forms of being in keeping with the principles of universal order, whereas wood was considered capable of promoting new growth and tackling challenges. The element of air was defined as *ch'i,* the cosmic breath infusing all of creation, and hence does not appear on the wheel shown in figure 3–1. It does, however, combine with other elements to produce such tangible realities as weather:

$Ch'i$ + fire = heat
$Ch'i$ + metal = favorable conditions
$Ch'i$ + earth = wind
$Ch'i$ + water = cold
$Ch'i$ + wood = rain

South
Red
Fire
Public face

Green, purple, red
Wealth / Abundance

Red, pink, white
Relationships / Marriage

East
Green
Wood
Family /
Health

Center
Earth
Yellow

West
White
Metal
Children /
New ideas

Black, blue, green
Knowledge / Self-Nurturing

White, gray, black
Benefactors / Travel

North
Black
Water
Career

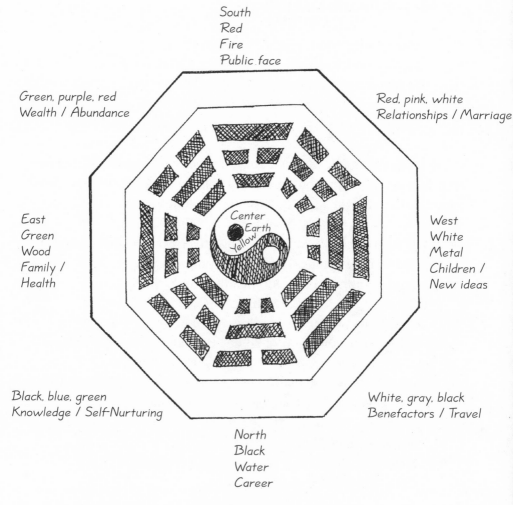

Figure 3–1  Chinese bagua wheel

The directions and colors on this wheel are rooted in Chinese astronomy and astrology, which view the four primary directions as divided by four great constellations: the red bird (or phoenix) of the south, the white tiger of the west, the black tortoise of the north, and the green dragon of the east. Based on this cosmology, the ideal site in China—and throughout the Northern Hemisphere—is one that opens to the south, where solar gains permeate the living space. The directions correlate with the following features:

> South—fire, noon, awake, summer, yang
> East—wood, evening, slowing time, autumn, yin
> North—water, midnight, sleep time, winter, yin
> West—metal, dawn, newly awakened time, spring, yang
> Center—earth, day and night, timelessness, yin and yang

The colors play an integral role in *bagua* interpretation, because each hue emits a vibration and tone of its own. Properties associated with the six true colors of Buddhism are as follows:

> White—metal/alchemy, beginnings, the moon, mourning, the lungs
> Red—fire, weddings, happiness, yang, the heart
> Yellow—imperial splendor, earth, center, the spleen
> Green—hope, new growth, spring, wood, the liver
> Blue/Indigo—heaven, sky, mourning
> Black—a combination of all colors, endings, yin, the kidneys

The *bagua* wheel depicted here contains three additional colors which, in traditional Chinese medicine, are linked with these properties:

> Purple/Plum—respect, great fortune
> Pink—joy, gentle and pure feelings, romance
> Gray—a blending of opposites

The facets of life corresponding to each segment of the *bagua* wheel originate in the folklore that was compiled as feng shui came into being. The ancient Chinese were wise and practical people. They knew that human beings can easily lose sight of essential aspects of personal existence. Unattended to, these parts were believed to float out of reach into the air around people's heads, producing a sense of overwhelm. To avoid such occurrences, the ancient ones assigned these facets of human life to areas of the environment, where people could direct a clear *intent* toward them and create harmony both without and within. Such laserlike focus on career, knowledge/self-nurturing, family/health, wealth/abundance, public face, relationships/marriage, children/new ideas, and benefactors/travel does indeed give rise to miraculous transformations!

With the *bagua* elements, directions, colors, and life motifs so intimately woven into the terrain we inhabit, our job is simply to alter our environments in keeping with their energies. In some instances, this may mean accentuating their impact; in others, it will mean counteracting imbalances. Always, human intention is the healing factor.

To experience the flow of *ch'i* in your home or work space, observe how you move within it. Are your movements smooth and fluid, or do you feel pressed and harried, or cramped and likely to trip over things? In other words, is *ch'i* flowing freely or is it too concentrated, or somehow obstructed?

Even before entering a building, feng shui practitioners study this flow of *ch'i*. They walk the neighborhood, evaluating currents of energy as well as yin and yang forces exerted on the site. They know, for example, that low-lying gently rolling hills and valleys tend to be yin in nature. They are aware that sharp peaks such as those in the Olympic Mountain Range in Washington state, the Grand Tetons in Wyoming, and the Rocky Mountains in the Southwest are strongly yang. And they are keenly attuned to the fact that landscapes in which neither yin nor yang dominate are most conducive to inner balance.

Using the *bagua* wheel as a guide, you can assess the layout of *your* plot of land—and from there, the interior of the structure it supports. As you become more experienced in working with this wheel, you will discover a variety of tools to use in adjusting the earth's energy as it passes through your dwelling. Under the guidance of Gaia, you are likely to find that *any* space can be transformed from a racetrack into a congenial gathering place, or from a dead zone into an area pulsing with life!

## A Feng Shui Assessment

Each building is a being unto itself and must be treated as such. This belief is foremost in my mind as I conduct an assessment.

I usually start off by journeying shamanically to the building and communing with it, undistracted by the energy of its human occupants. (For a practice in journeying, see page 99.) The building always has a great deal to tell me, such as where to find congested spots from which energy must be "cleared." I also drive around the area to note the geographic features, health, and general conditions of the neighborhood or the surrounding terrain; the more environmental "layers" I take into account, the more knowledge there is to work with. Returning to the building, I study the entry point, viewing the street as yet another "door," and I evaluate the flow of *ch'i*. Only then do I begin a physical assessment, laying the *bagua* wheel over a drawing of the area. Sometimes I'll stretch the wheel over the city or state boundary to gather as much information as possible.

After evaluating the terrain, I turn my attention to the floor plan of the house, diagramming the structure as I walk through it. Upon completing the assessment, I compile a list of problems, solutions, and enhancements. I then furnish either a written assessment or an audiotape of the walk-through, depending on whether the client learns best by seeing or listening.

Let's assess a house belonging to a physician who is a national radio and television personality. First, we'll look at the plot of land on which it is situated (see figure 3–2). The land is rectangular and quite even in shape, which is very good in feng shui. The overall footprint of the house itself forms a zigzag, known in feng shui as a lightning shape. Provided that arms of the zigzag are of equal length, this design signifies auspicious power. Here, however, they are of unequal length, and as you can see, there are voids, or pieces missing from the footprint, in the areas of wealth/abundance and benefactors/travel. The solutions I proposed during my walk-through of the house appear later in this chapter.

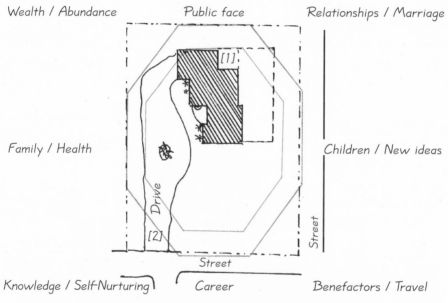

*Wealth / Abundance*　　　*Public face*　　　*Relationships / Marriage*

*Family / Health*　　　　　　　　　　*Children / New ideas*

*Knowledge / Self-Nurturing*　　*Career*　　　*Benefactors / Travel*

Figure 3–2  *Plot plan with bagua wheel overlay*

There is another difficulty too: the street behind the house is a busy thoroughfare. The rushing energy moving along this street can pull life-giving *ch'i* away from the house. To guard against this occurrence, I suggested placing plants, trees, or a wall in the area marked [1]. Had the occupant been a tenant rather than the home owner, or been unable to afford additional landscaping or construction, I would have advised buffering the home by placing an "intention" held by a rock or statue in this area.

A third difficulty with this plot of land is the culvert that passes beneath the driveway [2], accelerating the flow of fast-moving water. Vegetation planted here would serve the dual purpose of absorbing excess moisture and preventing the runoff of vital forces from the area of career.

Now let's explore the floor plan of the house, shown in figure 3–3. As before, the bracketed numbers in the text refer to the bracketed numbers on the floor plan. We will travel clockwise around the wheel, starting at the entry—the "mouth" of the building. Beginning here will help us see how the nourishing flow of *ch'i* moves into the body of the home. The healthier this nourishment, the healthier the home.

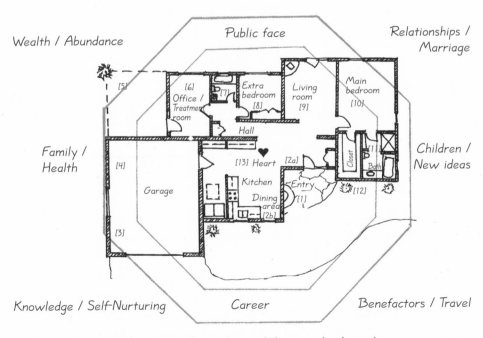

Figure 3–3 Floor plan with bagua wheel overlay

## [1, 2a, 2b] Career: Water

In this house the entry [1] is in the area of career, the facet of life in which energy is usually expended for monetary remuneration, and in turn, physical sustenance. The entry is marked by a beautiful, clean stone patio graced by a fountain. Double doors—allowing an abundance of *ch'i* to flow into the house—are painted turquoise, an excellent color for spiritual attunement, healing, and cleansing. Turquoise is also believed to protect property by shielding it against accidents and intruders.

The entry has two problems, however. The first is that the fountain isn't working and the water is stagnant—a situation to be quickly rectified or careers may be affected. This problem is particularly acute because in feng shui water represents career. In fact, I often recommend either a fountain or images of water at the entryway to a building, whether or not it is in the career area, because water is teeming with life.

The second problem here is the front patio's proximity to the drive. With no layers of separation between the two, the patio is overly exposed to passing vehicles. To remedy the situation, I suggested installing beside the front door a statue of a guardian animal, such as a foo dog, tiger, or other fierce protector.

The area inside the entry works well. A spacious vestibule opens onto an airy hall [2a] with tall ceilings. The floor is tiled and covered by area rugs that define the space and provide grounding. Immediately evident in the hall is the home owner's harp, augmenting the sense of harmony and gentle resonance. Close by is the kitchen, well situated here since homemaking is at least as much a career as any outside the home. The kitchen windows, as well as those in the adjacent dining area [2b], are good for career, as they form an opening for the incoming flow of *ch'i*. And they are well-sized—not so small as to restrict this inward flow and not large enough to invite its immediate departure.

To enhance your own career, be sure to focus on the area of your home or workplace aligned with the bottom of the *bagua* wheel. If you are seeking a promotion or a transfer to a different sphere of responsibility, this is the place to display an image of yourself or someone else performing the new work. Whatever you choose to exhibit here, even if it is nothing more than a small stone, will carry your intention for a thriving career.

For such purposes a traditional feng shui practitioner might recommend flutes or a mirror, but if these objects have no significance for you, choose something that does. Although objects carry a power of their own, the intention invested in them often has an even greater energetic influence. Intentional objects, because of the personal energy they hold, can release blocks to harmony, balance, and vitality.

### [3] Knowledge/Self-Nurturing

This area, compromised by the attached garage, suggests that knowledge and self-nurturing reside outside the main living space. In addition to limiting these aspects of the occupant's life, the attached garage poses other problems. Lead that settles on her shoes and clothing after she turns off her car engine is carried into the home where, once airborne, it may be inhaled or ingested. Other toxic fumes and chemicals also enter the home through the garage. A detached garage, on the other hand, would have allowed much of this toxicity to be deposited outside the home.

To incorporate knowledge and self-nurturing into the footprint of the house, I suggested that the garage hold objects representing the client's desires in these areas, whereupon she chose a lounge chair invested with her intention for fun and relaxation. Had the house been under construction, I would have advised placing objects permanently into the foundation or slab. One woman who did everything with gusto, set so many objects into the forms for the footing of her house that the subcontractor objected, saying, "Madam, you are compromising the integrity of this foundation!"

### [4] Family/Health: Wood

This area, too, is in the garage and hence beyond the main body of the house—a situation likely to induce alienation from the family and to compromise the occupant's vibrant health. To encourage a harmonious family life, I advised her to fill this part of the garage with happy pictures of her interacting with family and friends. "If you have no happy pictures," I said, "draw them—even stick figures will do, for it's not so much the rendering as the intention that counts!"

To activate good health and vibrant well-being, I recommended the addition of a silk plant inside the garage and living plants along the outer wall. (For a listing of plants that absorb toxic chemicals, see page 121.) Bamboo, with its many varieties of luxuriant growth, is highly effective in such places, and can be contained if planted in a metal box.

Water placed in this area of wood will nourish its attributes; however, too much water, as in the case of a bathroom with several faucets, may only drown them. The most favorable solution is the addition of plants that will soak up excess amounts of moisture.

## [5, 6] Wealth/Abundance

The area of wealth/abundance encompasses two portions of the house. One is a void [5], where I proposed building a stone or straw-bale wall to convert this portion of the property into an outside room with a garden. A sturdy tree planted in the upper left corner of the garden, I explained, would aid greatly in drawing in a flow of abundance, as would the image of a turtle—a strong, steady, long-lived amphibian—to represent the long, steady flow of wealth. If a wall were not affordable, I would have suggested a garden bordered by rocks.

If you are struggling with a similar problem, remember that there are as many solutions as there are people to arrive at them. Trust your intuition!

The office [6] is well placed in this area of wealth/abundance. To further compensate for the void, I suggested displaying on the wall bordering it a deity such as a Hindu goddess or the god Ganesh, or as before, the image of a turtle. The large windows along the adjacent wall admit a prodigious flow of *ch'i,* yet risk having it leak *out* through the huge openings. To prevent a depletion of this life force, I advised softening and slowing its escape with curtains, drapes, or a stained-glass piece in the window, since *ch'i* is attracted to movement, color, light, and beauty.

## [7, 8, 9] Public Face: Fire

Having the bath [7] in the area of public face could be problematic, for no one wants their fame flushed down the toilet! To offset the likelihood of "fame drain," I advocated for life-filled plants. In other homes free of children, I have advised clients to suspend firecrackers over the toilet. Such problems call for "explosive" solutions!

The good news is that the toilet is against an inside wall. Too often, toilets back onto an outside wall for easy ventilation; but the downward pull of *ch'i* resulting from flushing along the periphery of the building tends to leach out vital forces. If your toilet is beside an outer wall, be sure to counteract these undesirable effects with a strong representation of upward-moving energy, such as an upward-growing plant or a photograph or mobile of birds. To find the best solution, rely on your intuition.

Here the guest room [8], with its door facing away from the rest of the house, offers a delightful sense of privacy yet suggests a hard-to-access public face. To enhance the home owner's expertise as a public speaker, I suggested a wall display of a great orator or a collage of audiences enjoying a presentation. By then, she was well aware that the intention behind the images is what provides fuel for manifestation.

The living room [9] is an ideal setting for the public face area. Although this woman spends quiet, intimate time in her living room, it serves as a "public" space as well. Use of the fireplace in the corner can add a burning vigor to her public image—a passion all the more pronounced since fire is the feng shui element for this aspect of life.

## [10] Relationships/Marriage

This placement is advantageous for the main bedroom. To help the room feel as safe and warm as possible, I proposed a rose scheme with a touch of forest green. For happily single people, it is often beneficial to adorn this area with a devotional image such as one of Kwan Yin, Chinese goddess of infinite love and compassion.

If you are interested in developing a significant relationship or are in the process of doing so, record your intention for what you want in a partner and place it in this portion of your home. Or draw up a list— the more clearly defined, the better—remembering that Spirit is exceedingly literal. Be careful about what you ask for, as energy moves and manifests very quickly!

If you wish to deepen your marital bond, this is the spot for doing so. If you are in the process of seeking a divorce, place your intention here for a smooth and loving transition. Above all, opt for harmonious relationships with the people in your world, especially yourself.

## [11] Children/New Ideas: Metal

The bathroom is a fine spot for bringing extra *ch'i* to new ideas. I advised placing an image of new projects here—in the form of a simple drawing, or even a small stone. Anything that serves as a reminder of a work in progress can prove enormously fruitful.

If you have children, this would be an ideal place for their bedrooms or playroom. Be careful not to display outdated pictures of them, however, for this may only keep you—and them—focused on the past. (Save the baby pictures for the family/health area.) If you are trying to become pregnant, this is a good place for images of robust, happy babies or newborn greeting cards or flowering bulbs. Be creative here, and have fun!

## [12] Benefactors/Travel

The area of benefactors/travel, which extends beyond the footprint of this house, needed to be brought in. As a solution, I advised setting statues or symbols of benefactors on the premises, such as Buddha, St. Francis, Kwan Yin, angels, or even helpful, supportive individuals. A benefactor is a being on the physical, mental, emotional, or spiritual plane who provides aid. Westerners, caught up as we are in seeking independence, often forget to ask for help. Yet no sooner do we call out for assistance than we find our lives teeming with invaluable friends, guides, and mentors.

In this area, as in all others, nothing remains static. Hence, any time an intentional object begins to feel outdated, be sure to replace it with one that keeps the desired energy moving. A benefactor who guides you through high school may no longer be of assistance when it comes time to take a job. Let your outer environment keep pace with your inner one.

This is also a good area for displaying pictures or postcards of places you would like to visit. Don't be surprised if travel plans to these destinations suddenly materialize!

## [13] Heart/Center: Earth

This is one of the most important areas of a building, for if the heart is unsettled, weighed down, or boxed in, it can affect the entire structure and its occupants. The heart of this house, situated between the hall and main entry, is subjected to an accelerated flow of *ch'i,* which may eventually give rise to insomnia, nervousness, or heart palpitations in the occupant. Fast-flowing *ch'i,* like a river in a deep canyon, is apt to sweep away everything in its path. It can even take one's breath away.

The solution recommended in this instance was to place stones, or images of strong, grounded energy such as mountains or land forms, in the central hallway to slow *ch'i* down enough to linger in the heart area. An area rug colored in earth tones can also decelerate the streaming of *ch'i* as it passes through a hallway. Long hallways such as those found in offices often benefit from pictures on the walls, or from slightly recessed doors. Because *ch'i* is attracted to beauty, color, sound, and movement, alterations of this sort can provide "staying power," effecting a more gentle, serpentine flow of energy.

If the heart area in your home or work space is weighed down, consider adding wind chimes, angelic statues, or upward-growing plants to lift and disperse the energy. A heart area boxed in by storage rooms or closets, on the other hand, is apt to be burdened by a slow-moving or nearly motionless flow of *ch'i,* known as *sha.* To offset the resulting stagnation, display images of clear, open vistas, such as views of a mountaintop, a meadow, or stars—all of which can help you connect to the flow of cosmic energy.

When the heart of your home or workplace is compromised in any way, all other areas can be adversely affected as well. So if you make no other changes in your environment this week, nourish the life-giving core of your world—*celebrate* it! Dress it up with a rose quartz heart, or even chocolate hearts, to infuse the atmosphere with sweet, steady, balanced energy.

Two additional situations can be addressed with the help of the *bagua* wheel: *unfriendly neighbors* and *psychic burglar alarms.* Living in proximity to others, you may at times feel threatened by a neighbor—in which case you would do well to reflect back the negative energies directed at you. This can be accomplished through a mirror that faces the offending party. If you share a wall with the offender, have the mirror face that wall; if the culprit lives downstairs, place it in an inconspicuous spot on the floor. Be absolutely sure to set the mirror in place with clear intentions for harmony, for any ill will on your part may reflect back to you in triple magnification!

Regrettably, some people walk the earth in a dark cloud, spreading negativity wherever they go. Bless them and send it back. For added protection, surround your home or office with a circle of light to help filter out nonsupportive energies.

Traditional feng shui burglar alarms run the gamut from "sealing the door" rituals to *mudras,* or hand gestures, for warding off evil. Ancient Celts, as we will see in chapter 5, were more likely to use signs and symbols for protection, which I am accustomed to drawing on doors and entry floors in either obvious or hidden places. In the end the best protection against robbery or injury comes from our core. The light and love we radiate repels harmful energies in our midst. When bad things do happen, our task is to see them not as victimizing, but as opportunities for growth.

No matter how well-designed your home or office may be, there is always room for improvement. But remember that too many feng shui books can "spoil the broth." Why? Because every feng shui practitioner, published or unpublished, will have a slightly different interpretation of the forces impinging on an environment. To achieve true harmony, rely on *your* intuition and call on your benefactors and guides for help. As in ancient times, this form of Chinese divination is most effective when practiced not dogmatically, but as joyfully and creatively as possible.

*Chapter Four*

# The Native American Medicine Wheel

*I circle around*
*The boundaries of the earth,*
*Wearing long wing feathers*
*As I fly, as I fly.*

—The Ghost Dance

The medicine wheel, according to Native American elders, is the hoop we live within on the spiritual plane when we are in balance and harmony. The more accustomed we are to its energies, the more likely we are to integrate its wisdom into our daily lives.

This wheel is mapped out in accordance with the directions and elements. Unlike the *bagua* wheel, it emphasizes the seasons of nature, times of day, animal people, moon seasons, life stages, and life paths. Traditionally, the interweaving of these energies leads to the understanding that a human life has many "seasons." Numerous stories describe these seasons in terms of age or time of day. Both concepts are incorporated into one of the oldest enigmas posed, the riddle of the sphinx: *What crawls on all fours at dawn, walks upright at noon, and has three legs at sunset?* From infancy to adulthood to old age and the need for a cane, a human being does indeed pass through a cycle of seasons!

Timekeeping in many indigenous cultures of North America is based on the yearly dance of the seasons. Entire tribes attribute their survival to Gaia's heartbeat which, season after season, carries them through crises. We, too, can learn to stop what we are doing and smell the air for signs of a sweet, gentle rain; listen to the crackle that precedes a bitter lightning storm; gaze at drying leaves against an impossibly blue sky; and feel the coming of snow by the chill in our bones. In other words, we can allow our senses, rather than a wall calendar, to tell us what time of year it is. Letting our body lead us into each season, instead of encasing ourselves in "business as usual," is one way to move more fully into the hoop of life.

## Special Characteristics

According to Native American teachings, we walk the wheel of life every day, every year, and throughout the course of our lifetime. In each instance this journey around the wheel leads us through space as well as time. It guides us from the east, with its breath of spring and energy of childhood, to the south, fiery like summer and teeming with adolescent vigor and growth, to the west, the autumnal region of adulthood and caretaking where we find our life purpose, and at last to the north, the place of the elders where waning physical forces give way to winter's proliferation of spiritual forces. At the hub of the wheel is Spirit, sun, and moon, around which all else revolves.

On the medicine wheel overlay, the four primary directions are often associated with the following general characteristics. (*Note:* on this wheel we begin in the east, place of the rising sun.)

East—air; spring; dawn; winged ones; new beginnings; waxing moon; child; self-discovery; path of the visionary

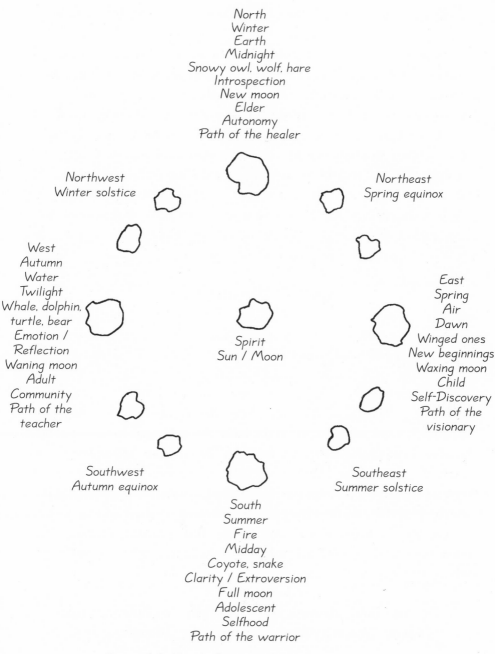

North
Winter
Earth
Midnight
Snowy owl, wolf, hare
Introspection
New moon
Elder
Autonomy
Path of the healer

Northwest
Winter solstice

Northeast
Spring equinox

West
Autumn
Water
Twilight
Whale, dolphin,
turtle, bear
Emotion /
Reflection
Waning moon
Adult
Community
Path of the
teacher

Spirit
Sun / Moon

East
Spring
Air
Dawn
Winged ones
New beginnings
Waxing moon
Child
Self-Discovery
Path of the
visionary

Southwest
Autumn equinox

Southeast
Summer solstice

South
Summer
Fire
Midday
Coyote, snake
Clarity / Extroversion
Full moon
Adolescent
Selfhood
Path of the warrior

Figure 4-1  Native American medicine wheel

South—fire; summer; midday; coyote, snake; clarity/extroversion; full moon; adolescent; selfhood; path of the warrior

West—water; autumn; twilight; whale, dolphin, turtle, bear; emotion/reflection; waning moon; adult; community; path of the teacher

North—earth; winter; midnight; snowy owl, wolf, hare; introspection; new moon; elder; autonomy; path of the healer

Center—Spirit, from which all life flows; sun; moon

The moon seasons shown on this medicine wheel are based on the thirteen moons appearing on the turtle's back—twelve around the outer edge of the shell and one at its center. Here only four of the twelve phases are noted, although you can imagine the others as you travel the wheel. These phases, even more so than each monthly moon, are reflected in a woman's menses and become known on a deep level.

The paths of the visionary, warrior, teacher, and healer are modern-day interpretations of life-phase purposes spelled out by Angeles Arrien, PhD, in her book *The Four-Fold Way*. They integrate ancient beliefs held by many indigenous peoples on the American continent.

## A Medicine Wheel Assessment

Let's use the medicine wheel to evaluate the two-story home of a family of seven situated on ten pine- and oak-studded acres high in the foothills of California's Sierra Mountains. The family designed and built the house themselves, careful to align it with true north and south. Such alignment provided full southern exposure to the sun's warmth and maximized the home's potential for generating harmony and balance (see figure 4–2).

The bilevel structure of the house will give us an added component to evaluate. In Gaiamancy, the stories of a building correlate with the

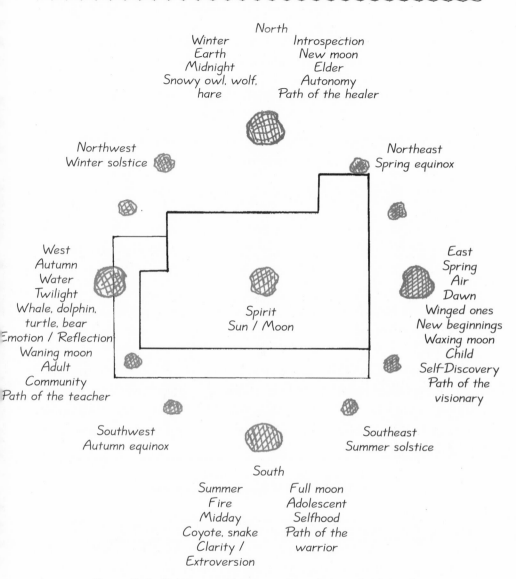

North
Winter          Introspection
Earth           New moon
Midnight        Elder
Snowy owl, wolf,  Autonomy
hare            Path of the healer

Northwest                              Northeast
Winter solstice                        Spring equinox

West                                   East
Autumn                                 Spring
Water                                  Air
Twilight                               Dawn
Whale, dolphin,   Spirit               Winged ones
turtle, bear      Sun / Moon           New beginnings
Emotion / Reflection                   Waxing moon
Waning moon                            Child
Adult                                  Self-Discovery
Community                              Path of the
Path of the teacher                    visionary

Southwest                              Southeast
Autumn equinox                         Summer solstice

South
Summer          Full moon
Fire            Adolescent
Midday          Selfhood
Coyote, snake   Path of the
Clarity /       warrior
Extroversion

*Figure 4–2  Footprint of house with medicine wheel overlay*

planes of human existence: the basement corresponds to the unconscious, the ground floor to the physical plane, and the second floor to the spiritual plane. The higher one lives in a building, the more grounding is needed to provide balance and contact with Gaia.

Our assessment of this house will begin at the front entry on the first floor (figure 4–3) and proceed to the second floor (figure 4–4). As in chapter 3, keep your own setting in mind, and enhance or troubleshoot using solutions that are meaningful to you. Be creative and joyful, all the while remembering that any object can be replaced as your circumstances change. Life is never static, and solutions should not be, either.

## First Floor

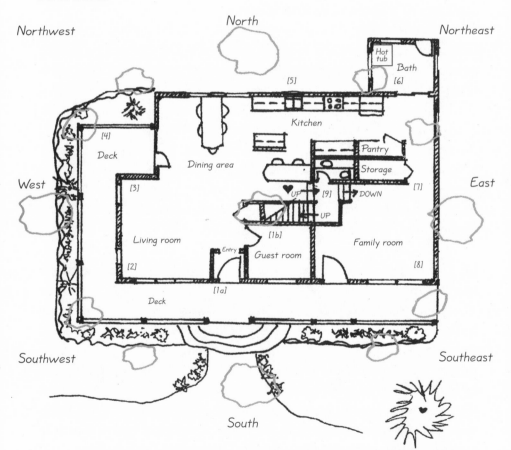

Figure 4–3 First floor plan with medicine wheel overlay

## [1] South: Fire, summer, clarity/extroversion, full moon, path of the warrior

A south-facing entry implies fullness of being, which for this home is accentuated by wide, welcoming river-rock steps leading to the front porch. The river rocks give an impression of solidity and longevity, as does the foundation, also built of stone from the nearby river. To help differentiate the main door [1a] from the door leading to the family room, I suggested placing plants on either side of it. I also advised replacing it with a wooden door containing a glass panel etched with a sun (fire) or a cornucopia (fruitfulness).

The entry hall, although small, creates a good airlock against the cold winter climate of the foothills. Because this is the area of fruitfulness as well as the "mouth" of the building, I emphasized the importance of bringing in golds and other rich colors.

The guest room [1b], too, is in the place of the south. Here I recommended the addition of a picture or object representing the path of the warrior—a path not of battle and bloodshed, but of courage, integrity, truth seeking, and the clarity to follow one's designated course. Even a stone imbued with intention could reinforce the power of living in truth and honor. Traditional Native American symbols of the south include corn, geese, and trout.

## [2] Southwest: Autumn equinox (September 21), waning three-quarter moon

The living room occupies this place of growth, self-expansion, and healthy maturation. To celebrate these harvest attributes, I proposed accenting this portion of the room with family photographs. Because there were teenagers in the family, I suggested adding representations of budding flowers to enhance their path to young adulthood. This is the place for gathering in and acknowledging the gifts that bring sustenance to everyone who lives in the home. Traditional Native American symbols of the southwest include deer, salmon, and brown bears.

## [3] West: Water, autumn, emotion/reflection, waning half moon, path of the teacher

The living room extends into the west, the place of adulthood, strength, and community. Continuing the deck around to this portion of the house was an excellent idea, for it invites family members to reflect on the gathering starlight and immerse themselves in the bounties of autumn—the reddening of the leaves, the crispness of the air, and the pungent aromas carried by the wind. Chairs arranged on the deck encouraged them to take in all these glories and the sunset as well.

Many Westerners have become so enamored of youth that they often forget the splendor, grace, and sweetness of the golden years. Hence it is important to celebrate this area of your own home or office with images of sunset beauty. Images of water and of autumn's soft, golden light belong here, too. Traditional Native American symbols of the west are elk, acorns, and sleeping trees.

## [4] Northwest: Winter solstice (December 21), waning quarter moon

Because energies of the northwest remain outside the house, its occupants are removed from the forces of winter solstice. These forces evoke an impulse to go into the darkness and prepare for new life, to experience the abundance that lies "fallow" in dark soil, and to take a respite from the busyness of the growing season. In other words, the darkness of winter solstice beckons us to be still and listen. It also inspires us to move into the dreamworld and help bring its energy to fruition.

While speaking with the family, I suggested ritualistically opening the dining room doors to the deck each day to welcome these energies back into their lives. The doors, however, were stuck shut, and the knobs broken—a situation requiring immediate attention. Always, our environment has a message for us!

I also proposed hanging lanterns on the deck to honor the importance of turning to the light for renewal, letting go of the past, and facing the future. Beneath the lanterns, the family set out a small potted evergreen plant to represent eternal life. Traditional Native American symbols of the northwest are tree sap, owls, and black bears.

### [5] North: Earth, winter, introspection, new moon, path of the healer

The kitchen occupies this site, which is auspicious in many ways. For one, the quiet restfulness of the season aids digestion. For another, the window faces a healing panorama of pine trees—tall green "standing ones" revered for their whisperings in the wind and for their sweetness of scent. In addition, the family is gifted with a lingering image of evening meals prepared here in the darkening hours, and of the warmth of food merging with appetizing aromas wafting up from the stove. My only suggestion was to counteract the fast-moving energy passing through the sink drain by filling the windowsill with clay pots of growing herbs to represent the goodness of earth's plants. Traditional Native American symbols of the north are storytelling figures, snowy owls, and wolves.

### [6] Northeast: Spring equinox (March 21)

Interestingly, there is a hot tub in this place of predawn and rebirth. Bathing here is therefore reminiscent of the sun about to glow on the horizon, announcing the arrival of a new day and a personal rebirth. The element of water further nurtures the budding time, which in this landscape will result in an abundance of daffodils, crocuses, and fresh grass. Traditional animal people equated with the spring equinox include frogs, hummingbirds, and otters.

### [7] East: Air, spring, new beginnings, waxing half moon, path of the visionary

A large portion of the family room is in the east, the place for shedding old skin and starting anew. Here the children spend time with one another and with their friends. To supplement the "kid energy" permeating this room, I advised each member of the family to contribute an item representing a project they hoped to undertake. Considering the significant amount of heat generated here by youthful energy, the wood-stove could conceivably "heat things up" too much; to balance the fire and sustain harmonious relations, I suggested adding symbols from the other three primary directions. Animal people for this area are hawks, eagles, beavers, and baby bears.

## [8] Southeast: Summer solstice (June 21), waxing three-quarter moon

The family room extends into the southeast, the portion of the medicine wheel that honors the day of longest light, celebrated for thousands of years as the occasion for late planting. This time of changing seasons was charted by the Sun Dagger site at Chaco Canyon in northwestern New Mexico—one of many wonders that attest to the midsummer shift in the sun's pattern. The family room, filled with the energy of this shift, is a place for fostering family relationships in a new way. Changes in family dynamics, as in cosmic ones, are part of the wheel of life, and our task is to learn to flow with them and grow without fear.

## [9] Center: Heart, sun and moon together

The heart of a home must, like the physical heart, be strong, steady, and able to maintain healthy circulation. In this home, however, it is not, for its action is compromised by the constant back-and-forth traffic in the hall, together with the up-and-down movement on the stairways. This fast-moving energy can contribute to nervousness, insomnia, and heart palpitations. What is needed are symbols of steady, grounded energy on the walls, such as photographs of mountains or images of serenity, peacefulness, and beauty.

In the center of my home, for example, is a lithograph of a heart-shaped plumeria lei resting on sand at the edge of the surf. For me, this image is steadying and grounding: the lei exemplifies the spirit of aloha's welcome and hospitality, its heart shape reveals beauty and grace, the aromatic plumeria remind me of Hawaii's warm heart, and the sandy shore is reminiscent of the healthy ebb and flow of life.

The bathroom at the center of the home in the Sierra Mountains is as problematic as the central hallway. Pipes can "drain" vital energy from the heart area; clogs, leaks, or drips are apt to have ill effects as well. Plants—or pictures of plants or flowers—would both uplift the energy here and promote good health.

## Second Floor

This portion of our assessment will address only the unbalanced areas of the second-story floor plan. (See figure 4–4.)

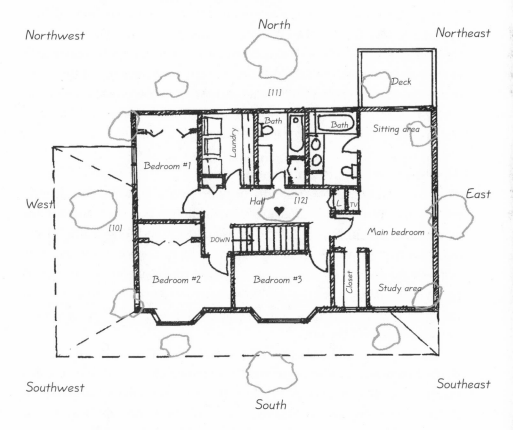

Figure 4–4 Second floor plan with medicine wheel overlay

## [10] West

This place of reflection, situated between bedroom #2 and bedroom #1, is "lost in the closet." To draw its influences into second-story living, I recommended hanging a picture of water, dolphins, or a sunset on the hallway wall.

## [11] North

The laundry room and two bathrooms occupying this area suggest that healing wisdom of the elders is "going down the drain." To offset such an effect, I suggested placing in each of these rooms at least one strong, upward-pulling image, such as that of a bird; eagles, redtail hawks, and owls, for example, possess enough wing power to counteract down-ward drafts. Since all these rooms have north-facing windows, low-light plants would help absorb excess moisture while evoking the promise of healing. Because the second floor is the spiritual level of the house, angel or avatar energy would also be effective here, as would images of Buddha, Mary, Kwan Yin, Jesus, the saints, or any other divine being.

## [12] Center

The heart area, composed of hallway and stairs, is once again compro-mised. Because the energy here needs to be grounded and steadied, the same solutions apply as before—namely, images of mountains, rocks, heart-shaped objects, even pyramids.

*Chapter Five*

# The Celtic Wheel

*I arise today through the strength of heaven,*
*light of sun, radiance of moon,*
*splendor of fire, speed of lightning,*
*swiftness of wind, depth of sea,*
*stability of earth, and firmness of rock.*

—Ancient Irish poem

The Celts originated in parts of Spain, Iberia, Switzerland, Germany, and Italy, and began migrating in large numbers to the British Isles between 2000 and 1200 BCE. As centuries passed, Germans, Saxons, and Anglo-Saxons pushed them out of the area now known as England, and as a result most people of Celtic lineage now live in Ireland, Scotland, Wales, the Isle of Man, Cornwall, and Brittany.

## A Brief History of the Celts

The word *Celt* (pronounced with a hard K) is Greek for stranger, but to the Romans it meant barbarian. One account, by first-century BCE Roman historian Pliny, tells of an encounter between Roman legions and Celts still remaining in Europe. The Etruscans, in northern Italy, had asked Rome for protection against the Celts after the Romans had broken a treaty guaranteeing a truce. In the ensuing battle, a Roman envoy named Quintus Fabius killed a Celtic leader, whereupon the Celts demanded justice. When it was not forthcoming, they marched against Rome, laying siege to the city for seven months—a campaign so successful that it ended only after the Romans paid them 1,000 pounds in gold. This series of events constituted the worst defeat the Romans had ever known, earning the Celts great respect as warriors and triggering a centuries-long Roman vendetta against them.

Long before the siege of Rome took place, even well before the first wave of Celts left their homeland in central Europe, the British Isles were occupied by Picts—small-statured, less aggressive people—and Tuatha Dé Danann, "people of the goddess Danu," who were believed capable of moving beyond the dimensions of time, space, and matter. The Picts, according to some historians, were the mythical "wee folk" described in legends. The Tuatha Dé Danann, tall and slender humans of great strength, superior craftsmanship, and advanced spirituality, are said to have intermarried with the Celtic arrivals, merging the wisdom and customs of both cultures. The Tuatha Dé Danann are considered the fourth group to have invaded the British Isles, and the Celts, or Gaelic people, the fifth. The crafts of the Celts included magical arts, wizardry, and metallurgy, as is evidenced in a variety of intricate and beautiful artifacts. Indeed, their artistry, knowledge, and spiritual practices are said to have rivaled those of contemporaneous Eastern and African cultures.

More information about the history of the Celts has been revealed by way of contact with other realms, but historians look askance at knowledge gleaned through such unorthodox methods. We do know, however, that the Druids—poets, teachers, philosophers, judges, doctors, and musicians of the Celtic tribes—were exceedingly well-educated. "Graduates" of schools for poets, known as shamans, they apprenticed for twelve to twenty years before going into communities to practice their arts. Unlike scientists who systematically observed the elements, or magicians who liberated the beings of the elements, these shamans *worked with* the elements, scrupulously studying them after taking on their beings.

I came to understand this shamanic way of knowing first as a child and later through more formal training. Knowing, in these terms, arises from *experiencing the inner reality* of the element, tree, or animal under consideration. For example, if I want to understand a particular body of water, I become a part of it; relying on my interconnection with the water, I move into its molecular makeup. This is not a matter of gazing at water and visualizing its composition; instead, it entails shape-shifting into the atoms themselves. (For a simple introduction to this method of acquiring knowledge, see practice 5 on pages 99–100.)

The depth of understanding achieved through Celtic shamanism is reflected in the intricate patterns and knotwork of metallurgic art, which in Gaiamancy forms the basis for the Celtic wheel (see figure 5–1). This particular wheel was adapted from the knot revealed in *The Book of Kells,* written in the twelfth century. The attributes ascribed to each of the directions required more intuitive "piecing together" than those appearing on either the *bagua* or the medicine wheel, because in China traits were written down early on and in North America they were carried forward in ritualized form, whereas in the Celtic world they remained more covert. Some of these attributes were derived from artifacts; others were inspired by Celtic legends and stories first recorded by Celtic Christian monks in the 1200s. The most famous of these, *The Book of Ballymote,* written in the 1300s, suggests—and archaeologists agree—that the Celts lived in close-knit tribal groups in such harmony with the land that in their view there was no separation between nature and people.

The Celts themselves passed on their practices through a collection of written symbols known as *ogham*—a twenty-five-character binary system of lines, each combination of which represents a tree or plant. This tree alphabet was used for divination, to seek guidance, and as a mnemonic device similar to the picture script of Egyptian hieroglyphs. The highly symbolic characters of *ogham* were relayed in secret communications from the time Celtic practices were outlawed by Rome until the early

1600s. Not until the 1700s were serious attempts made to decode these characters.

Going further back in time, the Druids, who developed the tree alphabet, did not document their wisdom, but rather passed it on orally in poetry, song, and master-apprentice transmissions. Utilizing *ogham* hand gestures and stone markings—a system far more cryptic than writing—was their way of safeguarding sacred knowledge from those who might misuse it. Curiously, the characters of *ogham* are similar to the symbols of the *I Ching,* suggesting another golden thread weaving together the manifestations of Gaia's wisdom.

## Special Characteristics

The lore transcribed by monks of the early Celtic church, together with the knowledge once locked within ogham and the practices of Celtic spirituality, find a home on the Celtic wheel. This wheel, like the *bagua* and medicine wheels, is arranged in accordance with the compass points and honors the elements and facets, or pathways, of human life. Unlike the other wheels, it commemorates festivals of the year, magical gifts, sacred animals, and trees, as outlined below:

> South—summer solstice, fire, path of fruitfulness and harmony, Sword of Finias, apple, horse
>
> West—autumn equinox, water, path of wholeness, Cauldron of Murias, alder, otter
>
> North—winter solstice, earth (stone), path of initiation, Stone of Falias, rowan, raven
>
> East—spring equinox, air, path of flexibility and fluidity, Spear of Gorias, willow, hare
>
> Center—the beginning and end of all paths, elder

Midway between each of these primary directions is a "point of crossing" in the Celtic knot. They reflect the turning points of the year, times when energies transition.

The festivals honored on the Celtic wheel commemorate the equinox and solstice, as well as the points of crossing. These include the celebrations of Lugnasadh, the sun god; Samhain, the Celtic New Year and Festival of the Dead; Imbolc, the Rites of Spring; and Beltaine, May Day.

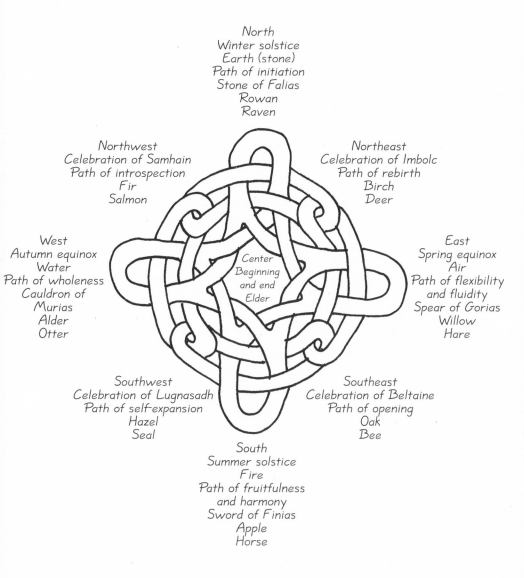

North
Winter solstice
Earth (stone)
Path of initiation
Stone of Falias
Rowan
Raven

Northwest
Celebration of Samhain
Path of introspection
Fir
Salmon

Northeast
Celebration of Imbolc
Path of rebirth
Birch
Deer

West
Autumn equinox
Water
Path of wholeness
Cauldron of
Murias
Alder
Otter

Center
Beginning
and end
Elder

East
Spring equinox
Air
Path of flexibility
and fluidity
Spear of Gorias
Willow
Hare

Southwest
Celebration of Lugnasadh
Path of self-expansion
Hazel
Seal

Southeast
Celebration of Beltaine
Path of opening
Oak
Bee

South
Summer solstice
Fire
Path of fruitfulness
and harmony
Sword of Finias
Apple
Horse

Figure 5–1  Celtic wheel

Each of the magical gifts appearing on the wheel was bestowed by a god or goddess on one of the four major cities of the Tuatha Dé Danann: Finias, Murias, Falias, and Gorias. Old Irish texts describe these cities as "otherworldly," explaining that the cosmology of the early Celts consisted of a *middle world* (the physical world), *otherworlds* (the worlds above), and *underworlds* (the worlds below). The Sword of Finias, to the south, was similar to King Arthur's Excalibur; its bearer was to be ever victorious in battle. The Cauldron of Murias, to the west, provided unending sustenance and reflected the future. The Stone of Falias, the northernmost city, was called the Stone of Destiny; this giant crystal ball revealed the past, foretold the future, and cried out in a human voice when touched by the rightful King of Erin. The Spear of Gorias, to the east, was Lugnasadh's lance, dubbed the "long arm" for his unerring aim.

The warlike gifts were more than mere weapons. They served to clarify and clear. For us, as for the early Celts, the Sword of Finias can be used to cut ties that are no longer needed. Likewise, the Spear of Gorias can be used to eliminate with a swift stroke those patterns that interfere with our balance and harmony.

Trees, another feature of Gaiamancy's Celtic wheel, were considered "people" with wondrous offerings. The ancient Celts' cathedrals were groves of trees; their schools of learning introduced the tree alphabet as a code for remembering complex information; and they lived by a tree calendar constructed in about 600 BCE. Certainly, the British Isles at the time were blanketed with magnificent, long-enduring forests. Oaks lived for hundreds of years; yews for thousands. The species selected for the Celtic wheel can spark memories of the knowledge held by the ancient ones, all the while transmitting important lessons in respect, honor, and the quiet art of listening.

Their English and original Gaelic names, together with their properties, are as follows:

Apple (*Quert*)—a tree bearing juicy, plentiful fruits that keep
    well into the fall and early winter. This tree provides both

food and graceful foliage, serving as a source of beauty for the soul. *Call on the apple for the sweet nature of its being, and for the gifts of abundance and juiciness.*

Hazel (*Coll*)—a bearer of insight. The Druids—knowledgeable as they were in surveying, measuring, and calculating—used hazel twigs while divining for water. Because of its pliant nature, this tree is also associated with mediation. *Call on the hazel for the capacity to see beneath the surface of things and for "divining" the true meaning of your emotions.*

Alder (*Fearn*)—a prolific, water-loving tree that grows with great gusto. This tree, often associated with the labyrinth, grants protection to those on the path of wholeness. *Call on the alder when you need support for quick growth and to fill a void in your life with beauty, grace, and regenerative powers.*

Fir (*Ailim*)—a tree that grows to great heights and confers healing effects. This tree aids in the ability to rise above surface features to acquire a more detached perspective. *Call on the sweet-scented fir when you want to extend beyond a hectic daily life to access the whisper of intuition.*

Rowan (*Luis*)—a tree with berries bearing a five-pointed star, or pentagram, ancient symbol of protection. Giant rowan groves on the British Isles were believed to provide sanctuary to the faerie people. *Call on the rowan when you are in need of a guardian.*

Birch (*Beith*)—a graceful, slender, water-dependent tree able to withstand extremely cold temperatures. Celts used the white bark of this twenty- to thirty-foot tree for making baskets and for starting fires. *Call on the birch for assistance in acquiring ancient wisdom through the purifyng process of rebirth, which on a cellular level can occur daily!*

Willow (*Saille*)—a tree that thrives near water and protects against disease by soaking up excess dampness caused by standing water. In *ogham* this tree represents the feminine cycles sacred to the moon goddess. *Call on the willow for support in transcending rigid behavior and ideas, bending with the "flow," and keeping your feet firmly planted when blows are buffeting you from head to toe.*

Oak (*Duir*)—a slow-growing species that develops a taproot deep enough to enable its survival in times of drought. *Duir* means solidity, and in fact this strong and beautiful tree was used for doors, furniture, and many house parts. *Call on the long-lived oak for steady, deeply rooted support while embarking on a new career, relationship, or other endeavor.*

Elder (*Ruis*)—a smooth-barked tree that in sheltered spots attains a height of over twenty feet. Known for its medicinal properties and its ability to grow in a great diversity of soils, this tree represents the thirteenth month in the *ogham* calendar and symbolizes regeneration. *Call on the elder when old and new come together, and you need assistance in releasing and welcoming.*

The animals on the Celtic wheel are drawn from the many guides and teachers active in the old Celtic world. Below are their English and Gaelic names, together with their attributes:

Horse (*Each*)—a guide to other realms. The Celtic goddess Rhiannon rides a swift white horse. And for millennia these animals have carried humans on their backs. *Horse will transport you to your destination—whether it is physical, emotional, mental, or spiritual—and will stand beside you as a friend.*

Seal (*Rön*)—an emotional ally. Celtic lore refers to *selchies* (silkies), seals that took on the form of women; while on land they kept their sealskins hidden for easy returns to the sea. *Seal will help you explore the depths of emotion and submerge, with trust, in the great unconscious.*

Otter (*Dobhran*)—the epitome of playfulness and joy. This animal makes a game out of any situation. *Otter will teach you how to play in lieu of being overly serious, and how to "let go" into the moment.*

Salmon (*Bradan*)—a conveyer of sustaining power. In Celtic legends this fish is gifted with the capacity to overcome major obstacles in its quest for the Source. *Fiercely intense, salmon will help you achieve all difficult goals.*

Raven (*Brän*)—guide to a clear, penetrating voice. Larger than its cousin, crow, this sage being—like coyote, pigeon, seagull, and others that thrive in our midst—is too often devalued and unrecognized for its gifts. *Raven will lead you to the universal unconscious and be your ally in times of darkness.*

Deer (*Eilid*)—embodiment of feminity, grace, and fleet-footedness. Cernunnos, the Greenman of Celtic lore, has horns like a male deer, and shape-shifters are often said to take on the form of a deer. *As you approach the heart of any forest, deer will hasten and support you on your journey.*

Hare (*Gearr*)—a teacher of quick and silent movements. This animal, which is larger and stronger than the bunny rabbit of North America, symbolizes creativity and the goddess. *Hare will present you with the "eggs" of rebirth and new growth.*

Bee (*Beach*)—a pollinator that brings new life to fruition. This insect aids in the reproduction of flowering plants and works cooperatively to produce sweet honey. *Bee will help you find work that keeps you "humming."*

## A Celtic Wheel Assessment

Using the Celtic wheel overlay, we will assess the floor plan of a condominium belonging to a young couple, both of whom have careers and see their home as a haven. The north- and south-facing walls are shared with neighboring dwellings (see figure 5–2).

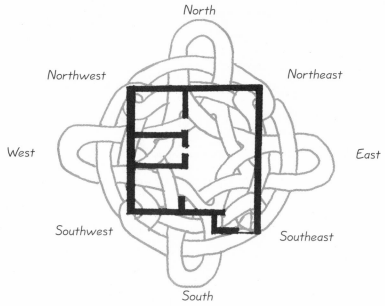

*Figure 5–2  Plot plan (condominium) with Celtic wheel overlay*

Entering the condominium through the front door in the southeast, we will proceed directly to the south and follow the wheel around clockwise (see figure 5–3). As before, keep your own home or office in mind while moving through this space.

### [1] South: Summer solstice (June 21), fire, path of fruitfulness and harmony, Sword of Finias, apple, horse

This area is the place where seeds grow into nourishment, abundance, and sustenance on all levels. The void you see here is problematic, for

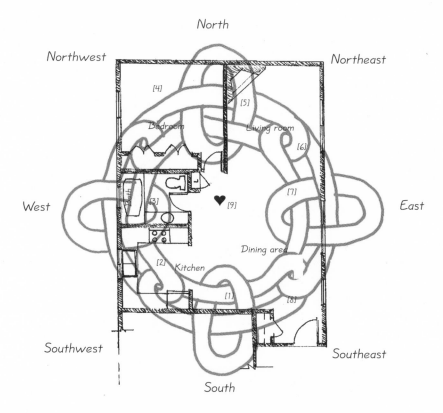

*Figure 5–3  Floor plan with Celtic wheel overlay*

the lost space must be reclaimed without infringing on the neighbor's energy. A picture displaying images of abundance might be helpful, but pictures and mirrors can create "windows" to the other side of a wall, which in most instances is not advantageous.

I suggested placing a small table against the shared wall, holding objects representative of abundance and fruitfulness. The couple wanted to hang a nature scene above it. To avoid letting it create a window, I advised them to draw an ancient Celtic symbol (see figure 5–4) on the back of the picture. This symbol, which originally sig-

*Figure 5–4  Celtic symbol of protection*

nified the triple goddess in Celtic spirituality, was later adopted by the Celtic church as a sign of the trinity. Used anywhere protection is needed, it is of special benefit while traveling, or even when shipping packages.

Because of the condominium's lack of south-facing windows, I recommended amplifying the intention of fruitfulness with symbols of a generative career, since it is through daily work that gains are acquired on the physical, emotional, and mental levels. Images representing fruitfulness and harmony can be as simple as flower seeds in a beautiful bowl. The apple tree, too, can be called upon as a potent life symbol here, as can the love, loyalty, and carrying power of horse.

### [2] Southwest: Celebration of Lugnasadh (July 31), path of self-expansion, hazel, seal

This area marks the time of long summer nights, the harvest, and marital as well as community formation. It is also about raising the young, cultivating a sense of family working together, and working things out together in the spirit of cooperation. What a perfect place it is for the kitchen—a room designed for family nourishment! To further enhance the effects of growth and cooperation, I proposed adding objects that suggest a rich harvest, such as baskets of fruit, dried gourds, and garlands of garlic.

What does this place of self-expansion offer in your home or office? Does it sustain you in growing and stretching? Does it help you feel supported, and supportive, in family life? ("Family" can mean you and your partner, you and your children, or you and your goldfish or plants.) If enhancement is needed, consider an image of the hazel tree, a small bowl containing a handful of hazelnuts, or a sculpted seal to help you move smoothly into community outreach.

### [3] West: Autumn equinox (September 21), water, path of wholeness, Cauldron of Murias, alder, otter

The season of the west extends from the autumn equinox to the Celtic

New Year of Samhain, celebrated on October 31. It is a time to reap what we have sown and to prepare for the slower, quieter, and more introspective dark months.

The element here is water, hence it is a prime location for the bathroom, where the order of the day is soaking, slowing down, and cleansing. Bathing in this area of the cauldron is equivalent to immersing oneself in the cosmic womb, holding-place of the feminine. To help the couple embark on the path of wholeness, I advised setting a bowl filled with special stones on the counter, further honoring the wisdom and holding power symbolized by the cauldron of the ancient city of Murias. I also suggested that they draw on the alder's energy here to counteract the downward-pulling currents passing through the drains.

## [4] Northwest: Celebration of Samhain (New Year—October 31), path of introspection, fir, salmon

The area of Samhain, marking both the New Year and Festival of the Dead, serves as a reminder to prepare for cold, wintry weather. Ancient Celts believed this festival ushered in not only the "death" of the previous year but also their chance to help spirits of the dead move on. Such assistance was made possible by a "thinning out" of the veils between realms that occurred at the end of the month we know as October, inviting communication with ancestors and others; the thinned out veils increased the possibility of communicating with ancestors and otherwordly guides. The Celts also regarded this as the time most conducive to shape-shifting, or taking on different physical forms such as those of animals.

Because the opening between worlds frightened many Christians, Samhain eventually transformed into Halloween, or All Hallows' Eve— a time for dressing up as skeletons and ghouls, reminiscent of the dead, and journeying into the night to beg for sweets. In the ninth century, the Catholic Church retained vestiges of Samhain with its inauguration of All Saints' Day on November 1, when saints come out at midnight to drive the restless dead back into their graves and the demons back into hell, and of All Souls' Day on November 2, to honor the dead. Today, children in Catholic school honor the dead on October 31 by lighting candles in church, attending Mass, then dressing in scary costumes and going out into the night. Moving into the darkness in this way symbolizes the deepening of introspection.

The bedroom in this condominium is perfectly situated to foster the internal focus of the northwest. To enhance the experience even more, I advised the couple to honor their ancestors by placing photographs or objects reminiscent of them in this sacred space; to adorn the room with a miniature fir to keep the occupants receptive to the soft whisper of intuition; and to hang a painting of a salmon to assist them in surmounting seemingly impossible obstacles. The path of introspection leads directly to personal accountability, recognition of one's own sacredness, and ultimately the path of initiation to the north.

**[5] North: Winter solstice (December 21), earth (stone), path of initiation, Stone of Falias, rowan, raven**
This place of stasis, stillness, and silence is the home of Cernunnos the Greenman, also known as the horned one, or Pan. Believed to have lived long before humans appeared on the planet, he was of otherwordly realms, whereas Falias was of the Tuatha Dé Danann. The word *Falias* comes from Faland, the northernmost city in the Celtic British Isles, known for the passing on of wisdom and learning. Hence, the north is where one goes for wisdom and counsel, both of which are gleaned through intuition. Those who take the journey are on the path of initiation.

The north is good placement for a living room with a fireplace. Why? Because winter solstice, the shortest day of the year, is when bonfires were lit to welcome the return of the light despite months of cold that still lay ahead. Cozy, safe, and warm, the occupants of this condominium can gather round the fire for storytelling, all the while distilling sparks of ancient wisdom.

To encourage their longevity and grace in aging, I advised this couple to call on the rowan. Like the cedars of Lebanon, these trees could be seen from the sea long before landfall. On their own, the couple opted to display a picture of raven here to protect their living space.

**[6] Northeast: Festival of Imbolc (January 31–February 1), path of rebirth, alder**

Here one emerges from the darkness and into light once again—a passage commemorated by the Festival of Imbolc, honoring the Rites of Spring. The following day, February 2, pays homage to Brighid, daughter of the Dagda, the all-father Gaelic god of the earth who in Christian lore is known as St. Brigit. Symbolizing the maiden spring's ability to overcome the waning hag of winter, Brighid is protectress of herd and stock, for this was the beginning of lambing season. Birches, too, are known for their protective qualities on this path of rebirth; after dying, they regenerate the forest with the richness held in their bodies.

The portion of the living room that extends into the northeast pays homage to the coming of new light, ideas, and ways of being. To accentuate it as a safe haven, I suggested filling it decorously with symbols of new growth in all areas of life, and calling on Brighid for aid and healing. Deer, the benefactor in this area, was evoked to help imbue it with a homelike feeling.

**[7] East: Spring equinox (March 21), air, path of flexibility and fluidity, Spear of Gorias, willow, hare**

The east is ruled by Gorias, spear of Lug, the sun god. The warrior who holds this spear wins every battle as a result of sureness of aim in the face of opposition. Here, too, is where the alchemy of metal, as seen in the spear, takes place—where elements are brought together for the creation of new matter. The predominant element for the east, however, is air. Streaming in with the air of spring is a sense of *inspiritu,* inspiration, being in spirit. In Celtic divinatory systems this place of emergence from the long winter months is symbolized by lambs, eggs, and the magical hare, harbinger of spring.

As the living room sweeps around to the east, it opens to the infant energy of the spring equinox, replete with budding, glorious sunrises, and hope for the coming year. To accentuate the use of lessons learned in dark times, I proposed adding enlivening images of the willow in the reborn world. This tree can convey lessons in maintaining flexibility while under pressure.

## [8] Southeast: Festival of Beltaine (May 1), path of opening, oak, bee

The southeast honors the joyful, sensual, playful celebration of Beltaine, or May Day—a time for fun, dance, and sexuality. The Maypole itself demonstrates a blending of the phallic and the round, woven together through ribbons of life.

With the dining room occupying this area, it is well suited for celebrating Beltaine's radiance through color and images of dance, food, joy, and brightness. I emphasized the theme of roses for honoring this path of opening, a fertile time in life. I advised the couple to call on bee, guardian of the southeast, to show them the way to the honey-laden hive. I also accentuated the importance of using the dining room for planting seeds of ideas and dreams, since here they can ripen.

In the southeast portion of your home, you may want to add an oak "dream box" to hold notes of the visions you would like to manifest. The steady, dependable oak can be counted on to hold fast to your hopes and dreams. While using such a tool, be sure to continually renew your aspirations, keeping the box fresh.

## [9] Center: Heart, the beginning and ending of all paths, elder

Here spirit rules. According to Celtic mythology, anyone traveling the labyrinth is approaching the heart of the goddess and releasing stagnant energy.

Such a task is easily accomplished with this floor plan, since the central area is quite open. To prevent the doorway to the bathroom from disturbing the heart area, I suggested hanging a picture of a forest on an adjacent wall or placing a small wooden table against it, representing the Tree of Life.

Remember to keep the heart of your own setting equally clear and flowing. Think of traveling to the heart of Gaia as you set your intention on cultivating a healthy, steady, loving heart for your home or workplace.

# Part Two

# Setting Forth

## Chapter Six

# *Relating to the Elements*

*Like Merlin*
*Would I through the forests spin.*
*What the storms are blowing,*
*What the thunders rumble,*
*What the lightnings mumble,*
*What the trees are speaking*
*When they're creaking,*
*Would I, like Merlin, be knowing . . .*
　　　　　　　　　　　—Lenau, "Merlin"

One of the best ways to deepen your work with the wheels is by developing a relationship with the elements at work in each of their segments. Most Western geomancies view the elements of earth, air, fire, and water as the building blocks of all physical life on our planet; other cultures, such as the Chinese, add to these the elements of metal and wood. Chemists, after breaking down the primary building blocks, arrived at a table of 106 elements, each of which expresses life's desire for oneness. These elements are composed of protons, electrons, quarks, and the "nothingness" between them, which forms the true source of life.

We are intimately connected with the elements, for they exist within as well as outside of our bodies. Ancient Maya cultures went so far as to refer to humans as "animated earth." Thinking in these terms, we can almost see our bodies rising from the land and, atom by atom, transmuting into flesh and blood—a bone here, sinew there—as the elements shaped themselves into portions of the human organism.

While familiarizing yourself with the elements, you may begin to wonder: Am I *this* intimately connected to the cosmos? The answer is yes. In fact, as your understanding of the elements unfolds, you will most likely be able to see, hear, and touch the spirits of earth, air, fire, water, metal, and wood—beings who out of their bountiful love have lent you a body through which to experience life on earth. The stone people, plant people, winged ones, and four-leggeds, too, have been physically created by the elements and are therefore allies equipped to assist you in your quest for balance and harmony.

The material that follows will help you relate more deeply to the elements. In time, you will be able to *feel* how *ch'i* impacts on your environment and ultimately affects the subtler energies of your being. These sensations can help guide you while reconfiguring a room, relandscaping your yard, or tackling a knotty problem at your entryway. The more you allow yourself to be informed by them, the more you will be raising your physical mental, emotional, and spiritual levels of vitality and well-being.

### Earth

> In clarity of clear crystal
> In depth of dark rock
> In weight of the world's matter
> In moulding silent stone
> In bones of the bare globe's darkness
> Is built Earth's form.
>
> —Lenau, "Merlin"

Did you know that about 33 percent of all human beings live in earthen structures? Or that human bone, muscle, organs, tissues, and skin are composed of the same substance as the earth? Certainly, it is tempting to adhere to the textbook notion of the earth as an inanimate body circling through a mathematically ordered solar system devoid of life. But the reality is that we are living on Gaia's body and deriving sustenance and form from her bounties!

In developing a relationship with the element of earth, begin by reconnecting with the spiritual forces of Gaia. These, after all, are what you will be communicating with as you walk the land you steward, assessing its strong and weak points. One way to meet with the spirit of Gaia is to ask permission before setting foot on your plot of land, as shamans of Old Hawaii did before entering a forest or jungle to "talk story" with the green people or to gather medicinal plants. In exchange, it is important to leave a small gift such as a handful of seeds, a strand of hair, or even spit. Also observe these common courtesies while collecting plants or stones, or digging in the soil.

Failure to establish this sort of give-and-take relationship can interfere with your ability to learn from the element of earth, as it did for a woman who once asked me to perform an assessment of the home she shared with her husband. When I perform an assessment, I mediate between people and their environment, although my intention is ultimately to step out of the way. So I spent several hours in this couple's home on different occasions, all the while talking with the spirits of the land, the house, and the couple's benefactors and guides. I then sat down with the husband and wife to relate what I had learned and pass on many of the suggestions I had been given.

The woman argued with me about every one of them. Nonplussed, I attempted to clarify the information, but to no avail. I finally realized that not only was I doing all the work but she was resistant to the "earthiness" of my interactions with the environment. She went so far as to tell me that anything of the earth was "unspiritual" and that I needed to go up to an angelic realm to find "real" answers.

I am ever grateful to this couple for the lesson they taught me—

namely, that the illusion of humanity's "taintedness" arises out of a fog born of people's fear and greed, and not of Gaia herself. The point is that the answers I was given *were* real, and turned out to be enormously helpful, as yours will be, provided that you honor the resources in the land beneath your feet.

In addition to asking permission and leaving a gift of gratitude, you can connect with the earth through gardening. Working in a garden fosters a humming way of being. The slow, rhythmic movements help you enter into a state of consciousness rich with information. Whether you are raising food for your family on a quarter-acre of land, cultivating a bed of herbs on a small city lot, or growing potted flowers on an apartment balcony, your interactions with the earth can bring you more than dirt under your fingernails; it can fill you with sweetness, pleasure, and wisdom!

A third way to access immediate information from your plot of land is to place on your finger a dusting of earth from an undisturbed place, such as under a rock or tree, and dabbing a tiny bit of it on the tip of your tongue. Tasting the soil will tell you whether it is sweet or sour, rich with energy or depleted of life forces. Use of the tongue, with its reliable powers of discernment, is a surefire way to establish a cellular bond with the land and the guardian spirits that reside there.

Many babies stuff fistfuls of earth in their mouths, often with great gusto. While they are eating the dirt, eager to experience a connection with this element, their mothers run over in a panic to stop them, setting in motion a concept of earth as "dirty" and "bad." I must admit that I, too, behaved like this when my son was young. It takes great self-control to avoid contributing to the pervasive fog in our midst, but little tastes of your own will help, and will give you a sense of the world that is hidden in a grain of sand.

The more often you interact with the earth, the more likely you are to develop a sensuous relationship with her soil. You may come to love the smell of it—especially after a rainfall, or while walking in a forest blanketed with rich loam. At times you may feel compelled to reach down and pick up a handful of topsoil, or run your fingers through the silkiness or chunkiness of its particles. For some people, seeing, hearing, tasting, smelling, or touching the earth sparks an ecstatic experience; for others, it evokes a deep sense of contentment. In both instances, the resulting state of being awakens a new awareness of interconnection with this glorious element. To deepen the awareness you achieve, work with practice 2.

*Practice 2*

## Connecting with the Spirits of the Land

Here is a ritual that can be performed on every plot of land you inhabit, whether it is covered by lush vegetation or asphalt and concrete: *create an altar to the spirits of the land.* Honored by such a sign of recognition, respect, and good neighborliness, these spirits will guide you in assessing the land and in fashioning the most harmonious environment possible. They are eager to be of service, to be benefactors to you and your family, or business associates; they ask only that you be a good neighbor and friend.

The altar you make can be as simple as a single stone or as elaborate as you choose. What matters most is the intention you bring to it. For example, the land I steward is overseen by a variety of special stones, a statue of Kwan Yin, and a Buddha. For your altar you might prefer a figure of Mary or St. Francis of Assisi, or beautiful pieces of wood. Whatever you decide on, invest it with good intentions, and each time you see it, know they will be reinforced.

Rather than using objects revered by other cultures, use what resonates for you—and trust your instincts! As important as it is to be honoring and respectful of ancient ways, it is just as crucial to personally delight in the connection you establish with the spirits of the land.

## Air

> Rolling in air-borne currents
> Whirling in hurricane's wrath
> Whistling in the winter's wind
> Rustling on a breeze's breath
> Rushing through the raging storm
> Breathes air's freedom.
>
> —Lenau, "Merlin"

Air is breath. Without it, we can survive for only a few minutes. Air breathed in brings life-giving oxygen to our cells and bloodstream; air breathed out is a "giving back" to the cosmos, a way of commingling our beingness with that of all others.

Air is also wind, breath of the planet. When the breezes quiet down, doesn't it feel as though the planet is holding its breath? When the wind is in motion, on the other hand, anything can happen: it may caress us, wrap itself around us, or blow us off our feet. Most often, the wind is friendly toward humans, and when asked for help it will cooperate. If you step outside and begin talking to the wind, it may come to you and softly touch your face, swirling gently around you like a faithful companion.

Because the element of air is invisible, some people have difficulty understanding it. A good way to get to know it is by watching birds fly. In the spread of their wings you can almost see the currents of air passing over and under each feather. Birds have a close partnership with air—a fact I discover anew each day I travel from my island home a few miles off the coast of Washington state. One of the many delights of living on an island is the need to ferry to the mainland, and among my greatest cruising pleasures is watching seagulls escort the ferry to its destination. As they fly in front of the captain's window, leading the way, they seem to take pride in their self-chosen responsibility, and joy in utilizing the air currents.

Another way to come to know air is by breathing more expansively. We in this culture tend to limit the flow of air into our lungs through shallow breathing. Contributing factors include our fast-paced lifestyles and the constrictive clothing we wear, such as neckties and chokers. If you feel a desire to breathe more freely and to better access the wisdom of air, try practice 3. With experience, you can become acutely aware of not only your own breath but that of the planet, and of the universe as well.

*Practice 3*

## Full-Belly Breathing

Practice this exercise daily to increase your lung capacity and to connect with your breath.

~ Sit erect, with your shoulders relaxed. Take a slow, deep breath, bringing the air in through your nose and all the way down to the bottom of your lungs, relaxing your belly outward.

~ Hold your breath for a few seconds before slowly releasing it, allowing your belly to move back inward.

~ Inhale, hold, and exhale six more times. If at any point you feel lightheaded, breathe normally for several minutes before returning to full-belly breathing.

~ When you are comfortable with this practice, add the following visualization: Imagine that with each inhalation you are breathing in infinite love and blessings, and with each exhalation you are releasing them into the universe as *your* blessing.

## Fire

Fury of enfolding flames
Flight of their dancing forms
Heat of the heaven's sun
Fire of its celestial sphere
And the seed's shoot springing towards the spreading sky
Flame with fire's force.

—Lenau, "Merlin"

Fire fuels our organs, warms our breath, heats up the blood in our veins, and regenerates our trillions of cells. From the fire that sparked creation to the flame that joins egg and sperm at the time of conception, this element has imprinted itself on human memory. And our knowledge of it is ongoing, for our planet, conceived in fire, is continually reshaping herself by releasing molten rock. Although fire's power to consume often frightens us, many ancient cultures equated it with purification. Some even envisioned the human heart as an organ of fire pumping cleansing flames throughout the body.

I learned of fire's purifying capacity in the summer of 1995, when my father passed on and was cremated. I returned home from the funeral to find myself in charge of a large burn pile on the land I was stewarding. The heavily forested acreage was being cleared for buildings and a ceremonial space, hence the fire was quite large. As it burned, I danced with the elements—the fire raging hot as could be, the air feeding it while generating energy of its own, the earth supporting it and keeping it contained, the water sizzling in the wood. I even danced with the water I was spraying around the periphery to keep the flames from spreading. At times the fire became so hot I asked it to please calm itself, and it was most responsive. While tending the burn pile for four days and nights, I bonded with the element of fire and began casting old, pent-up emotions and resentments into the flames. As I watched them being consumed and transmuted, I felt a profound sense of release.

This experience was doubly healing, since I'd had a fear of fire as a child, having been badly burned at age two.

To discover for yourself the awesome spirit of fire, call on the power of Pele, Hawaiian goddess of fire and volcanoes. Seek out her assistance any time you need intense cleansing energy to burn up emotional "garbage." But watch out! Not only does Pele transmute old life into new, but she is a fierce protectress—as many travelers discover after taking her lava rocks home with them. Every week, visitors bureaus of Hawaii receive hundreds of pounds of returned lava rocks!

Another way to experience the spirit of fire is to breathe into your cupped hands and feel the "flames" of your breath. Or try standing in the warmth of the sun. As you do, be sure to give thanks for the life support this burning being sends to us here on Gaia.

## Water

> The leaping, lashing ocean's swell
> The lapping, lulling ripple's wash
> The glistening, swirling rapid's flow
> The tumbling, twinkling, falling drops
> And the still lake's sunlit silence
> Weave the water's world.
>
> —Lenau, "Merlin"

Water is another of our longtime companions. Between 75 and 90 percent of the human body consists of this element; morover, we live on a water-based planet. The movement of the tides, ocean currents, rivers, and streams is in a sense no different from the ebb and flow of fluids in our own bodies. Water also cleanses and anoints us, first as newborns and again upon our death.

I, for one, have rarely lived more than a few hours from a body of water. I grew up along the Pacific Ocean and went on to live near the Atlantic Ocean as well as the Mediterranean, Aegean, Adriatic, and

Ionian Seas; I have also settled by rivers, lakes, streams, and healing springs. Indeed, most of our major cities are on or near water. Evidently, our ancestors instinctively knew what science has since proved—namely, that moving water, through negative ion activity, reduces anxiety and depression, especially winter depression; increases cognitive abilities and energy; and improves sleep. Circulating water also enhances air quality and helps neutralize stress, fatigue, illness, loss of concentration, weakening of the immune system, and other ill effects of operating electromagnetic devices that output positive ions. If you work in front of a computer for long periods of time, for example, you can help dispel any resulting lethargy or disorientation by placing a small fountain in your work space.

To deepen your relationship with water, you can always spit; if nothing else, this may reassure you that your own "well" is full. To experience the influence of water in your environment, relax with your eyes closed beside a pond, river, lake, or ocean. Breathe in the water molecules and feel the subtle effects of the moisture on your skin and on your emotional state. If you are near lapping waves, you may slip into a waking meditation or even fall fast asleep. The yin energy of water, although feminine, profoundly affects both men and women.

## Metal

> Look, it cannot be seen—it is beyond form
> Listen, it cannot be heard—it is beyond sound
> Grasp, it cannot be held—it is intangible.
> These three are indefinable
> Therefore they are joined in one.
> —Lao-tzu (570–490 BCE), *Tao Te Ching*

Compared with earth, air, fire, and water, the element of metal is less familiar to Westerners. According to Eastern beliefs, metal is the "offspring" of a blending of two or more elements, which is why on the Chinese *bagua* wheel children and metal occupy the same place. Some metals, however, are viewed not so much as their own "being" but rather as the blending itself.

Chinese medicine depicts alchemists as metal beings intent on observation, studiousness, and analysis. Interestingly, European and Middle Eastern alchemists who worked with this element were said to transmute base metals into gold, all the while accelerating processes already present in nature. Metal, in many alchemist traditions. is often symbolized by a rock, the large mass of strong material from which it is extracted, calling to mind the enigmatic philosophers' stone sought by European alchemists of the Middle Ages. Was this "stone" a symbol of spiritual transformation or was it conceived of as something more tangible, such as the transmutation of earth into metal? One helpful way to think of metal is as a synthesis of old and new into a separate universal creation.

To become better acquainted with the magic of this element, pick up a metal object and feel its texture and temperature, smell it, place it against your cheek. Also try to tune into the metal in the jewelry you wear, and in the snaps, zippers, hooks, and eyelets of your clothes. Chinese doctors believe that metal impacts on the functioning of our lungs.

Once you have augmented your relationship with metal, feel free to ask it for information. In doing so, ask the metal how to strengthen your contact with Gaia.

### Wood

> Fibres of its roots
> Oak tree has unbound,
> Spreading underground,
> Thousand mouths feed shoots,
> Sucking life from secret wells
> While the trunk to heaven swells.
> —Lenau, "Merlin"

Wood, although we tend not to think of it as an element, is well-known to us. Thousands of products in our world have their origins in trees— from the clothing we wear to the shingles on our roofs and the pages of our books.

Two of the most prominent features of wood are its ability to hold up under pressure and its flexibility. Wood also thrives on challenge and is impulsive. Chinese medicine takes this understanding a step further by portraying wood beings as pathfinders and adventurers.

My own experience with wood goes back to childhood. From the time I was six months old until I was eighteen, I spent my summers camping among trees in the Sierra Mountains of California. These trees were the grandfathers I never had, giving me a safe haven and an abiding sense of love. Later, I lived for several years in a 100-year-old log cabin where I grew to appreciate the sturdy strength of this holding environment. While remodeling old houses and building new ones, I came to respect and even thank the "bones" of trees that could stand for thousands of years, retaining their beauty, then give themselves over to works of art.

Perhaps you, too, feeling the great debt we owe to trees, can learn to express gratitude to them. Have you ever wandered through an old-growth forest replete with ancient spirits that bore witness to more than you could imagine? Have you ever thought of trees as the planet's lungs, freshening the atmosphere while gracing the terrain with their dignity and kindness? The more you communicate with the spirits of wood, the more likely they are to let you know what staunch friends and protectors they are.

*Chapter Seven*

# Tuning into the Lay of the Land

*Here the vast Dragon twines*
*Between the Bears and like a river winds.*

—Virgil

In addition to the elements, the lay of the land—the topography, as it is often called—provides enormous amounts of information about a chosen site and its effects on the occupants. Chapters 3, 4, and 5 touch upon some of the wisdom that can be gleaned by surveying a plot of land. Here we will go into greater detail, exploring land forms and the energy lines that pass through them.

## Land Forms

Ancient Chinese, Native American, Celtic, and other geomancers often saw traits of mythic beings in the land they surveyed. Depending on its shape, a plot of land was frequently thought of as a mythological animal or spirit. Gaiamancy requires no familiarity with these associations; it simply requests that you ask the land itself about its nature and characteristics. When asked respectfully, most land spirits will be pleased to impart information.

You may learn, for example, that flat land with little variation has calm or static energy, and that a site marked by hills and valleys is energetically more intense. Cues transmitted by the land spirits, or sparked by the contours of the land, will let you know if your home or worksite is healthy and supportive of you. If it is not, you may want to redirect its energy flow, enhance its energy, or if need be, relocate. In each instance, you will have deepened your relationship with the immediate environment.

On Whidbey Island, a few miles off the coast of Seattle, Washington, we can see a prime example of a dragon land form (figure 7–1). When viewed aerially, the dragon shape is evident: its head is at the ferry dock in Clinton, its tail loops around Deception Pass in the north, and its spine runs along the ridge that vertically spans the center of the island.

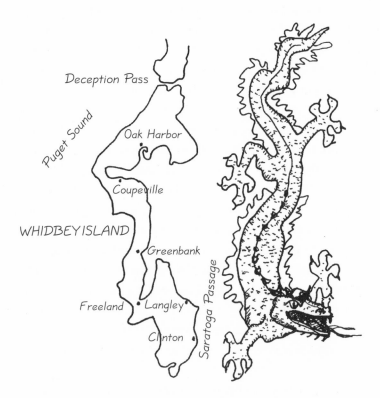

Figure 7–1  Whidbey Island as dragon

In numerous mythologies, the dragon—or green dragon, as it is often called in Chinese legends—is a potent being. Known for its longevity and versatility, it has the capacity to travel into the heavens as well as the earth, and to transmute negativity with fire.

On Whidbey Island the dragon demonstrates its many powers. The west side of the island is quite yang. Here the land is exposed to strong winds and storms coming off Puget Sound—a highway for international commerce, carrying large ships into and out of the ports of Seattle, Everett, and Port Townsend. Sure enough, the energy emanating from this side of the island is outgoing and public oriented, and the residents are for the most part gregarious. Facing west, these externally focused inhabitants look out onto the Olympic Peninsula's Hurricane Ridge, an inherently majestic range that displays even greater power through its mighty upthrusts.

The east side of Whidbey Island faces Saratoga Passage, whose waters are calm and gentle 90 percent of the time. Most of what is left of the island's old forests can be found here, giving off strong yet gentle feminine energy. The people who live on this side of the island are more reclusive, inner directed, and private, and the houses stand farther apart.

Along the central ridge of the island—the backbone of the dragon— you can see both Puget Sound and Saratoga Passage. The people who live in this energetically balanced area are dynamic and capable.

Throughout Whidbey Island, the dragon spirit is ever present. Powerful forces and personalities are apparent as soon as you set foot on the land, whether you have come in from the Clinton ferry, the Port Townsend ferry, or over the bridge crossing the turbulent waters of Deception Pass. The island has the dragonlike capacity to ascend to the skies by way of prolific populations of bald eagles, hawks, owls, and winged dragonflies; it can also burrow into the earth, as is illustrated by the profusion of greenery. The island's deep, mystical soul keeps its inhabitants earthbound and centered, while its environs transmute negativity with water.

Hawaiian mythology expands on this perspective. Here the dragon, known as *mo'o,* has played an active role in the life of the people, especially in pre-*ali'i* times, dating back to at least 1000 BCE. The *ali'i* were members of royalty appearing after the arrival of Polynesians. Attesting to its sustaining power, the word *mo'o* is sprinkled throughout the Hawaiian language: *mo'olelo* (history and traditions), *mo'olio* (pathway), *mo'oku'auhau* (genealogy chants), *mo'opuna* (grandchildren), *mo'owini* (vision), even Moloka'i (Island of the Dragon).

A representative of time, the dragon revered by Hawaiians begins in tomorrow (the head), the dawn of which is yet to come (the tail). Its body is said to characterize *o'hana* (the family). Its front feet are the *na opio* (the children), always restless, in motion, and changing. Its middle feet are *ka makua* (the parents)—foundation of the family and providers of food, shelter, and nurturing. The hind feet are the *kupuna* (grandparents), the strong stabilizers always ready to lend a hand. Forming the backbone behind the *kupuna* are the *ka iwi* (ancestors), who have passed out of the body and are available to offer protection and spiritual guidance. Each part, joining with the whole for fluidity of movement, depends on the others for balance.

## Earth's Energy Lines

Many types of energy lines pass below, around, and above the earth's surface, lending unique characteristics to the topography. Although all these pathways of invisible forces are generated by the earth herself, some were tampered with by earlier civilizations. The configurations most commonly known to transmit natural currents through the body of the planet are ley lines, dragon lines, faerie lines, ghost paths, and the golden grid. Below are descriptions of these energy conduits, as well as practical tips for working with them; for information on dowsing the land to locate energy lines, see pages 103–105.

### Ley Lines
Ley lines are naturally occurring underground pathways of earth energy. Wise ones of long ago, aware of the existence of these meridians,

sought to maximize their potency by tapping into them through standing stones and various other objects, as can be seen at Stonehenge and other ancient stone circles. Just as dams now harness the energy of rivers for generating electrical power, these stones were once used to amplify the earth's energy currents. Once intensified, the energy would come flowing forth, like a geyser.

Today, only portions of these intensified ley lines remain, some of which can be detected by following animal paths or tracks made by snails or snakes. The regrettable news is that knowledge of the earth's meridians has slipped into oblivion. The good news is that this wisdom is still accessible and simply awaits remembrance through our renewed partnership with Gaia.

## Dragon Lines

Known in China as *lung mei,* or dragon paths, these ripples of *ch'i* run both below and along the surface of the earth. Like wind currents, they are invisible yet powerful enough to profoundly affect a site or building, as well as its inhabitants. Underground dragon lines are comparable to ley lines: they can pool and become stagnant, or gather up speed, sweeping along everything in their paths. Lines on the surface of the earth, often called veins, are more easily detected. Some continue for long distances, whereas others stop and start, and can be found only in bits and pieces. I have also encountered lines that taper off gently, then suddenly end, as if they had plunged into the earth. Just as you would not place your home or business in the middle of a river, neither would you want to situate it along any one of these energy lines.

Until the twentieth century, most major buildings in China were constructed in such a way as to avoid the concentrated currents of energy traveling along dragon paths. Today, in places where this wisdom was ignored, feng shui practitioners are called in to make the needed corrections. They ensure, for example, that a strong dragon line passing through a building is rerouted, especially if it ends abruptly. Living over a suddenly terminating dragon line would be like teetering at the edge of a steep waterfall, where the powerful momentum of flow is most treacherous. If the line runs under a bedroom, the disturbance is most likely to show up in disrupted sleep patterns.

Although it is best to have a site dowsed before construction begins, modifications *can* be made later. When I find a preexisting dragon line, as I did in the house pictured in figure 7–2, I go to the point on the property closest to its source and, using metal bars, stones, or crystals, redirect the energy flow around the *sides* of the house; within safe proximity of the house, the two pathways will eventually merge back into one.

Most dragon lines will allow themselves to be redirected. When I meet up with resistance, I either set in place a rock willing to take on the dragon energy or display there the image of a powerful being capable of holding and absorbing the energy, such as Buddha or Kwan Yin or Green Tara. An image of Atlas, with the globe on his shoulders, would also work. Every culture, it seems, has at least one mythic hero or heroine willing to take on the task of holding weighty forces for the sake of a more balanced world!

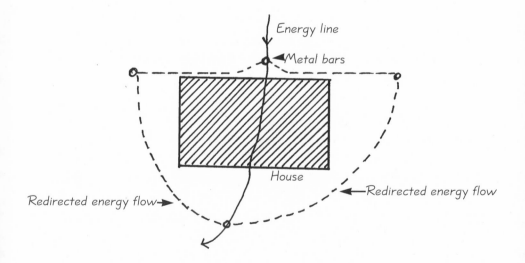

Figure 7–2 House with a redirected energy line

**Faerie Lines and Ghost Paths**

When faeries dance or travel, the lines they make can be extremely powerful. Ghost paths are more dangerous and are usually traversed only at night. Both types of pathways tend to turn, or even circle around, although some go straight up. Because it is unwise to obstruct these lines while faeries or spirits are using them, be sure to call in guides and helpers to counsel you on how to respectfully work with them. If you come across one of these lines out in the country, simply leave it alone; but if you find one in your home or office, call on the spirits of the land as well as your totem beings to help redirect it around the building.

**The Golden Grid**

The golden grid is an image given to me many years ago in a meditation. While sitting in silence, I was informed of a time when a visible web of golden threads encircled the earth, serving as a planetary immune system. This web, I was told, participated in the maintenance of balance and harmony on the earth. I have since heard others speak of a "harmonic device" that once surrounded Gaia, providing peace and safety to her inhabitants—a phenomenon closely akin to the golden grid.

People today can no longer see this sheath of light surrounding the earth. Why? Because having been penetrated and disrupted, it is no longer intact, and because our perception has dimmed with the passage of time. We can, however, reassemble it through intention, at once healing the perforated grid while cultivating an *inner* perception of its existence.

To envision the golden grid, picture a spiderweb enveloping the globe, its threads interlinked into patterns of grace and beauty. Imagine the web shining with dew, aglow with millions of points of sparkly light. Because of its delicacy, this grid is easily destroyed by pollution and the release of bombs, leaving Gaia's inhabitants increasingly vulnerable to forces of darkness. Yet each time we realign with the harmony of our surroundings, the grid is repaired and we move one step closer to planetary healing.

You may "see" the grid's golden threads reconnecting as you redesign your entryway to better conform with the earth's natural energy patterns. As you rearrange your living room, a glow may appear. Or while hanging a picture on your bedroom wall, you may suddenly feel a sense of well-being and an inner knowing that the golden grid is undergoing reconstruction.

*Chapter Eight*

# Putting Together a Tool Bag

*Concerning all acts of initiative (and creation), there is one elementary truth, the ignorance of which kills countless ideas and splendid plans: that the moment one definitely commits oneself, then Providence moves too. All sorts of things occur to help one that would not otherwise have occurred. A whole stream of events issues from the decision, raising in one's favor all manner of unforeseen incidents and meetings and material assistance.*

—William Hutchison Murray
*On the Scottish Himalayan Expedition*

The only skill needed for assessing the flow of earth energy through an environment is the ability to open the subtle senses. Yet when it comes to evaluating other energy flows, and certainly to correcting problems, a variety of skills and devices can be enormously helpful. With this in mind, consider filling a ceremonial bag with age-old tools of divination that you can reach for in times of need.

The tools described below are all associated with at least one of the three wheels of Gaiamancy. Feel free to mix and match them as you wish, combining the use of a feng shui device with a Native American discipline and a sacred object from the Celtic tradition, or whatever feels most natural to you. Interspersed among these tools are practices that, once tossed into your tool bag, can be used to enhance your perception.

## Intention

In putting together a tool bag for assessing your environment, begin with intention. This is the Gaiamancy tool par excellence, for only through intention can a solution become powerful enough to create an energy shift or a new form. Yet only through *clarity* can an intention work its magic. When an intention is crystal-clear, you can very quickly actualize your goal.

Along with clarity comes *responsibility*. Why? Because in effecting geomantic change, you will be entering into a cocreative relationship with *ch'i* and the elemental forces of life, and must therefore be accountable for the consequences of your decisions. According to the Tao, the world as we know it is pure energy, and it is our intentions that create our lives—a truth too often forgotten in Western cultures. Our tendency in the West is to turn our creative power over to an "expert" who will take care of things for us; but only when we reclaim that power, and take responsibility for it, will the hoped-for transformations occur.

I observed this natural law in action soon after a client eager to see dramatic changes in many areas of his life called me to perform an assessment of his office. A few days after it was completed, he phoned to say the changes he had hoped for were not happening, whereupon I met with him again and asked what his intention was. As it turned out, he thought *I* would bring about the changes for him. I explained that the service I provide enhances *his* intention, and that changes really were happening, beginning with his initial thought to call me. Once he understood the power of intention and surrendered to it, the universe brought about his desired changes—with results far exceeding his expectations.

I am in awe of my clients' courage to change. Often I will visit a home, walk through it, then go back to my office to prepare a written assessment. When I return to discuss it with my client, I invariably find that several of the solutions I recorded in the privacy of my office have *already been implemented.*

Here is another example of the transformative capacity of intention. If in the course of an assessment or a clearing you come across an energy that is causing harm, avoid engaging it with power. Instead, use intention to feel compassion toward it, then release it to the light. By being adversarial, you may only validate and intensify the unwanted energy, whereas projecting your love will neutralize it, rendering it powerless. This is not to say, "Turn the other cheek," but rather, "Be in your own strength." Tremendous power resides in pure intention.

The practice of Gaiamancy entails little struggle; it simply requires focus. The perceived need for struggle—a sad and strange fallacy in our culture—arises from the exercise of resistance and leads to disempowerment. Replacing "resistance against" an effort with "focus on" it can make all the difference in the world. So often we regard our lives as laden with hardship, when in reality a little more intention will give birth to miracles!

---

*Practice 4*

## Developing Intention

This powerful exercise actualizes intention quickly, so be clear and pure of heart each time you practice it.

~ Sit quietly, and breathe deeply seven times. Closing your eyes, allow your body to relax.

~ Choose an area of life you wish to enhance. Then call in your guides, angels, benefactors, or whomever you like to summon for support, and ask them to form a protective circle around you.

~ Imagine sitting in a bubble filled with golden light. Then state the change you wish to make, and ask for wisdom, guidance, continued protection, power, and clarity in bringing it about. (*Note: This*

*— continued —*

*practice is designed not to change another person, but rather to send your intention out with the highest integrity possible.*)

~ See the desired enhancement with your "inner eyes." If you are not particularly visual, *feel* the change.

~ Relax, let go of the wish, and again take seven deep breaths.

~ Slowly open your eyes and note any altered perceptions. If at first you notice nothing new, be patient. Because we are unaccustomed to the subtler aspects of being, we often need to practice clearing the mind, heart, and spirit before fine-tuning our intentions.

## Ritual

Ritual is intention brought into form. Any repetitive act that serves to affirm a symbolic connection to Gaia qualifies as ritual. In performing such an act, we establish a cellular memory bank of communion with divine powers, all the while grounding our statements of intention in the physical realm.

Many people have grown to resent the disempowering forms of ritual used by institutionalized religions; instead of feeling awe before the mystery and wonder of sacred acts, we often feel belittled by, if not fearful of, the clerics who perform them. Certainly, ritual has been used by religions to gain control over congregants and to establish a hierarchy of power. We must be careful, however, not to renounce ritual along with the elitism it has spawned, for the performance of sacred rites *in and of itself* is an essential means of linking back up with one another and with divine wisdom.

Following are forms of ritual that are likely to awaken ancient memories. They can also inspire a sense of community, ecstasy, and love.

### Repetitive Movements and Gestures
The ritual movements of dance, rattling, smudging, swaying, Tai Chi, and Qi Gong are potent vehicles for communing with Gaia. Dance with the moon, or the wind. Drum along with a thunderstorm. Invent your own physical movements for connecting and celebrating.

**Chanting and Singing**

Vocalizing—either out loud or telepathically—is an excellent way to communicate with animals, trees, and other beings. I have developed a friendship with a matriarch whale in Hawaii by silently singing to her while visualizing a communication link to her; I call it "talking story" to the whale, borrowing the Hawaiian term for conversation. Everything in the universe has a unique vibration that can be accessed through harmony and sound.

## Journeying to Other Realms

This form of communicating with beings in other worlds is sometimes called trance meditation or trance healing. It is a shamanic out-of-body travel technique used for either gathering information or acquiring clarity on a particular issue. Practiced originally by shamans intent on maintaining the well-being of their village, journeying has evolved into a more personalized tool for accessing guidance from other realms, as you will discover in working with practice 5.

*Practice 5*

## *Journeying for Information*

This technique can help you find answers to questions you may have about yourself and the space you inhabit.

~ With a glass of water beside you, sit or lie in a comfortable position, and close your eyes. Taking seven deep breaths, allow your body to relax completely.

~ Call in your guardian angels or whoever connects you with the divine, and ask for their protection throughout the forthcoming journey.

~ Now think of a question you have about yourself or your environ-

*continued*

ment. Keep it direct and free of "what ifs." For now, merely formulate your question.

~ As soon as you feel surrounded by a circle of protection, picture a real or imagined place in nature, then go to this place and sit comfortably. Take in the sights, sounds, smells, and textures of the setting.

~ Ask for a spirit guide, in the form of an animal or a divine being, to come and lead you on this journey. (Remember that you are protected and safe; if at any time you feel discomfort, know that you can open your eyes and return to your body.)

~ When the spirit guide appears, ask your question clearly and simply, then listen for an answer.

~ After you have received an answer, thank the spirit guide for its assistance. Now see yourself standing up, turning around, and coming back from this place in nature. Feel your spirit filling your body from the tips of your toes to the ends of your fingers and the top of your head. Then slowly open your eyes. You may feel extraordinarily energized and lucid, or perhaps a bit sleepy and spacey; in either case, slowly acclimate yourself to your surroundings.

~ For grounding purposes, take a drink of water, and allow a few minutes to pass before getting up and going about your day.

It is a good idea to record each of your journeying experiences in a journal or notebook. Also consider working with a teacher to help you process these experiences. Journeying is a profound practice best launched in the company of a knowledgeable mentor.

## Totems and Guides

Even without journeying, we can consult beings in other realms, especially totems and guides. Totem beings are most often animals, some of which are with us for life; guardians of our family group, these totems come to us at birth and reappear whenever their attributes are needed. Others visit for a period of time and then leave. Totem animals of both sorts bring spiritual assistance, wisdom, protection, and power.

Many times, we first see these animals repeatedly in books or films—some of their favorite ways to capture our attention. When we do not understand what they are trying to tell us, they can become exceedingly frustrated. Still, like patient friends, they will await a spark of recognition from us, as you will notice while working with practice 6.

The most common form of communication with totem animals occurs in visions and dreams. In fact, many aboriginal people believe that dreamtime is real and waking time the illusion. Totemic communication also takes place in our everyday waking states. In both instances these animals may take on an exaggerated or odd-looking appearance. One little creature in my circle of totemic friends, for example, resembles a cartoon character. I laughed when he first came up to me, then I realized I had offended him and quickly apologized, promising not to be patronizing or judgmental. This small being has taught me to be quiet and to view life from an inconspicuous vantage point.

Totems are sometimes referred to as "power animals"—an accurate description, for they literally embody powers and strengths for us. Native Americans often carry an image of the animal whose characteristics they wish to take on for hunting, healing, or overcoming a physical or emotional challenge. Yet totem beings are not restricted to the animal kingdom; they can also be trees, rocks, or other helpful inanimate forms. Members of the Catholic Church regard the relics of saints in much the same way that "pagans" view their totems.

Guides are less tangible cosmic beings who can be called upon for spiritual assistance, wisdom, guidance, protection, and power. Appeals to Mary are popular in Ireland and in Hispanic countries where, beneath the devotion to the Holy Mother, there often lies consultation with a living goddess. In other cultures the great mother goddess Kwan Yin of China or Rhea of Greece are invoked to offer the protection, compassion, and infinite love of the divine feminine. Similarly, Jesus and Buddha are beloved bearers of the divine masculine.

Can you recall an animal, member of the plant or elemental kingdom, or more cosmic entity that has been with you since childhood? If so, write a poem or letter to this being—and don't be surprised if it talks back! Conversing with totems and guides is a great asset in Gaiamancy, since their access to nonphysical realms is often far more direct than ours.

---

*Practice 6*

## Meeting Your Totem Animal

~ With a glass of water beside you, sit comfortably in a chair or lie on the floor. Closing your eyes, take a few deep breaths and relax as fully as possible.

~ Imagine a circle of golden light surrounding you. See or feel yourself inside this golden orb, and know that you are safe and protected by it. (If you feel uncomfortable at any point on the ensuing journey, simply open your eyes and allow your traveling spirit to reenter your body.)

~ Follow the pathway you took in practice 5 as you made your way to a special place in nature. As soon as you arrive, seek out a guide in the form of a physical being or a presence. Ask the guide to lead you to your totem animal.

~ Follow the guide to a real or imagined meadow, cave, mountaintop, forest, or seashore—all the while seeing, hearing, and smelling the newfound world around you. Your totem animal will be there to greet you; acknowledge it as an ally and friend.

~ Ask questions of this totem and find out how long it has been with you. It may say that this is its first time meeting you, or that it has

*continued*

been with you since birth, or in previous lifetimes. When your questions have been answered, thank the totem and say good-bye. Then ask your guide to escort you back to the pathway.

~ Follow the pathway to your point of origin. Then return to your body, taking time to let your spirit fill it inch by inch before slowly opening your eyes.

~ Take a drink of water, and wait several minutes before diving back into ordinary reality.

Once you have come to know your totem animal, you will no longer need to search for it. On the contrary, the animal will begin to show up in your day-to-day life—and when it does, be sure to greet it with a sense of recognition and receptivity.

## Dowsing

Dowsing, in one form or another, is used in almost every world culture to detect the site of water, objects, or energy lines beneath the surface of the earth. The word itself, derived from an old Anglo-Saxon word meaning "to push down," refers to the original device used by dowsers. After cutting a Y-shaped branch from a tree, often a willow, they would hold the ends of it and take note as the stem eventually turned downward over a sensitive location. Dowsers today use a forked twig, metallic rods, or a pendulum of metal, bone, or stone.

A dowsing rod is a valuable addition to your tool bag. Why? Because it can help you locate water for wells, or underground streams or rivers that might otherwise impact on your environment. It can also be used to trace septic systems and electrical lines. Some people even dowse *on a map* for oil, gold, or minerals. Others dowse for missing people, or downed planes or boats.

Subtle energy lines are responsive to dowsing, too, as are areas of geopathic stress. Left alone, slight geologic shifts will, like energy lines, either push up against the foundation of a building or pull it into the earth. Once detected, the responsible energies can usually be worked with if approached with an attitude of respect and cooperation.

I learned how to dowse from an old fellow in Oregon who came to the land I was building a house on. Calling himself a "water witcher," this vintage dowser arrived with two rods made out of bent coat hangers and proceeded to walk the acreage and mark off two places for a well site. As it turned out, both the depth for the well and the water quality he reported were exactly right! But best of all, he showed me how to hold the rods and how to ask crystal-clear questions.

Clarity is vital while using dowsing rods, for they interpret information literally, as I was to learn many years later. After laying electrical lines to several large buildings at a newly constructed spiritual center, my partner at the time spliced one of the lines and ran it to a smaller building, burying all the wires side-by-side deep in the ground. When the small building experienced a drop in power a few weeks later, we realized we had forgotten to mark the splice, which now, on a cold and wet December day, needed repair.

With great confidence, I whipped out my coat-hanger rods and proceeded to search for the splice. Finding the affected wire, I tracked its path, but each time I asked, "Where are the wires separated?" I received the same cryptic answer: "Two feet." In response, my partner dug two feet along the path, and then two more feet, until he had excavated nearly one-third of the original 200-foot trench. At that point, in utter frustration, we asked our Buddha-cat, Max, "Where is the *break?*" Max marched over to a spot, dug a little hole, and strolled off. My partner and I looked at each other and chuckled, then we dug down two feet at the designated place. Sure enough, there was the culprit! Never again did I ask a dowsing tool anything but clear, specific questions.

Since meeting the water witcher, I have used various dowsing devices—crystals and swivels, beads and bells—yet bent metal coat hangers from the dry cleaner are still among my favorite tools, since they are light and easy to balance for long spans of time. I also use brass welding rods of various lengths, and at times a pendulum—a great tool that fits in a pocket. I even have a set of pocket-size dowsing rods, each about six inches long!

Whichever device you decide to use, be sure to follow this simple method. When dowsing a site for water, energy lines, or electrical lines, begin by asking the land spirits for their permission, cooperation, and assistance; in exchange for their help, leave a small gift, such as tobacco or birdseed. Then holding your dowsing device straight out in front of you, ask them to guide you to the desired spot.

You may find that the tool you use responds differently in each situation. If while dowsing for water I use coat hangers or welding rods, they will often cross and wrap themselves around my neck. If I am searching for buried electrical lines, the rods will separate to the left and right. If there is an energy vortex, they will also swing away from each other. Asking questions as you walk, such as, "Where is the clean, potable drinking water?" will help clarify the search. By visualizing the water, you may even be able to see the rocks in an underground river, or the stones of an aquifer.

Once you locate water, traverse the area to find easy access to it. Upon detecting electrical lines, wind back and forth across the suspected trajectory to find their path. Remember that while walking the land you may encounter faerie rings—loops of energy left by dancing faeries. If you do, respectfully avoid passing through them. If you can find no way around them, warn the faerie people of your approach, and ask their permission before entering their domain. It is an honor to have these rings on the land you steward.

## Pendulums

Of all the divining tools, pendulums are among the easiest to use. Because the body of a pendulum is suspended from a fixed point, it will swing freely to and fro, proving yes-or-no answers to your questions. You need only be as still as possible and ask the questions.

You can either buy a pendulum or make your own. The next step is to decide which motion will signify a "yes" response, which one a "no" response, and which one a "maybe" response. For simplicity's sake, you may want to designate the forward-and-backward swing of the pendulum as yes, and the side-to-side swing as a no, like the "yes" and "no" nodding of the head; a circular motion could indicate "maybe." Allow the tool to tell you what is best.

Before using the pendulum, clear your energy field; this will prevent other forces from influencing the answers you are given. To clear your energy field, close your eyes and take several deep, slow breaths. Imagine that a rain of light falling over your body is removing all but the most beneficial energy coming your way. When you feel a sense of release and clarity, open your eyes and proceed.

To establish a wholesome camaraderie with your pendulum, hold it in your dominant hand above the surface of a table and begin to work with it. Relaxing your hand and keeping it as still as possible, ask a yes-or-no question that you know the answer to. If the pendulum does not move right away, patiently ask another question and see what happens. Communicating with subtle energies of this nature often takes practice. Try using your nondominant hand, too; this will cause you to use the side of your brain you're less accustomed to operating with.

### Sacred Objects, Cures, and Ceremonies

No tool bag is complete without an assortment of sacred objects, cures (the feng shui term for solutions), and ceremonies. Those listed below can be used for troubleshooting, either in conjunction with their respective wheels or separately. As always, strive for clarity of intention while applying these solutions. Also take a moment to thank the wisdom keepers who through eons of time have lovingly saved them from distortion.

These are only a few of the many sacred objects and practices employed by each of the three traditions. For more options, see the recommended reading list beginning on page 141. Above all, be discerning—fill your bag only with tools that are meaningful to *you*.

## Feng Shui Tools

The tools of feng shui are fairly universal and easy to work with. Listed below are the basic cures performed by the Black Hat school.

***Light-refracting objects, such as mirrors and crystals.*** Mirrors are used in feng shui to cure a host of design difficulties. Properly placed, they can deflect negative energy, connect the interior of a building to a space outside its footprint, and redirect the flow of *ch'i*. Crystals, good sources of light healing and energy, are also excellent for clearing negative energy and redirecting *ch'i*.

A *word of caution:* Please remember that although the effectiveness of these cures is influenced by the intention with which they are used, the objects have energies *of their own*. Mirrors, I have found, can open an energetic "window" between two spaces, which in many cases may be undesirable. Crystals, for their part, should be understood before being put to use. For knowledge of a particular crystal, clear your mind and ask your guides what gifts this crystal embodies.

***Sound.*** Wind chimes are good for dispersing energy. Solid chimes made of metal will send out concentric circles of *ch'i*. Hollow chimes of metal or bamboo are more apt to emit a protective wall of energy. Singing or chanting with purity of heart has the capacity to attract divine beings. Drums, whistles, and rattles also work well, as they shake up negative energies and release them vibrationally.

***Living objects.*** *Ch'i* is attracted to the beauty of nature. For this reason I often recommend the use of plants or trees to correct an imbalance either inside a building or out. In addition, many people like to place real or representational goldfish in their entryway to draw in energies associated with nature's abundance of water.

*Moving objects.* Items such as wind socks, weather vanes, windmills, and mobiles can help move stagnant *ch'i*. They can also disperse fast-moving *ch'i* as it travels down a long, narrow passageway.

*Heavy objects.* The weight of heavy objects helps to bring energy back to earth. *Ch'i* is often grounded by statues, stones, and such topographical features as mountains or pyramids. Cultures worldwide, including the ancient Celts, used megalithic stones as signposts to show the locations of ley lines, sacred sites, and healing springs.

*Electrical power.* Feng shui practitioners in China typically believe that machines represent great power. They regard electronic equipment as a sign of affluence and success. As an environmental consultant, I am a bit more cautious about the electromagnetic fields machinery generates.

*Flutes.* Currently a universal symbol for feng shui, flutes carry the ancient intention for musical harmony and beauty. When hung at an angle with the mouthpiece facing downward, they represent the potential for uplifting the surrounding energy through the power of harmony and rhythm.

*Colors.* The effects of individual colors are often dependent on cultural interpretation. White, for example, a color of mourning in China, is worn by brides in the West. Black, revered for its blending properties in China, is associated with mourning in the West. When using colors as solutions, the best approach is to trust your intuition. You can always ask your guides, or even a color itself, if it is right for a particular area and application.

*Others.* Personal cures for balancing the flow of *ch'i* can be as effective as traditional ones. I often use wildflower seeds, for example, since they are readily available and carry bountiful energy. After researching the characteristics of flowers you love and observing their distinct personalities, you, too, may want to apply this cure in the major sectors of the *bagua* wheel.

In the area of wealth/abundance, for instance, you may find that sunflower, fruit tree, or other seeds convey the energy of blossoming wealth and new growth, as well as the grace and beauty essential to true abundance. You could either plant these seeds to bring your intention to fruition, or simply sprinkle them in a basket and let them weave their magic. The area of relationships/marriage might benefit from sweet pea or carnation seeds, which represent love and romance. The family/health area might respond well to seeds or shoots of plants associated with robust health and vitality, such as bamboo. Augmenting the area further, you may want to add statues of elephants, traditionally revered for their strong family ties and long lives.

## Native American Tools

First Nation people, as a whole, make use of hundreds of sacred objects and customs to balance and harmonize the forces in their environment. Those listed below are among the most ubiquitous.

*Smudging.* This custom entails the burning of herbs, grasses, and leaves for clearing and purifying. The burning of sage is said to eradicate many diseases and serve as a drying agent for the body. Smudging with cedar sweetens. Sweetgrass is more clearing and grounding.

*Calling the circle.* This sacred ritual calls in the wisdom, guidance, and protection of the spirits of the directions. Calling the circle before performing a ceremonial clearing or balancing can help insulate the space.

---

*Practice 7*

## Calling the Circle

This ritual has similar counterparts in many cultures. It is used to preserve the safety of a space about to be healed.

~ Stand facing east, close your eyes, and call aloud to the spirits of the east—the area of new beginnings marked by the path of the visionary. Ask these spirits to bring their wisdom, guidance, protection, and power to the circle that will be formed.

*continued*

~ Turning clockwise, repeat the call, bringing in energy from the spirits of the south, west, and north, respectively.

~ Facing upward, call to Father Sky, Grandmother Moon, and Grandfather Sun to bring in their energy.

~ Facing downward, call to Mother Earth and ask her to bring in her energy.

~ Invite all the beings of purest intention and highest integrity to join the circle.

~ Acknowledge the presence of all the spirits in the circle, and welcome their wisdom, guidance, and protection.

~ When you have completed the work or healing you wish to do, release the spirits, thanking them for their love and support.

*Dance.* Because the body is vested with innate knowledge and wisdom, dance can "speak" in ways that words cannot. Actually, dance is one of the most powerful prayers there is, helpful in balancing the physical body as well as the surrounding energies.

You may want to perform a totem dance, in which you take on the physical characteristics of your totem animal or cosmic being—a profound way to connect with this being and kinesthetically learn about its gifts. Or you might prefer to choreograph your own dance by closing your eyes and simply allowing your body to move.

*Drums.* In Native American cultures drums reenact the heartbeat of the earth. Their rhythms are also used to send shamans into other worlds; in fact, the Ulchi and Nanai of Siberia believe that they "ride the drum" on their journeys. If you enjoy drumming, consider adopting this tool for entering an altered state or for clearing imbalances.

## Celtic Tools

Most sacred objects of the early Celts had their origins in legend and lore. Those described below are among the many that laid the groundwork for reestablishing healthy relationships with the world of nature and with beings in other realms.

*Crane bags.* In Celtic shamanism, crane bags hold the sacred tools used in the practice of medicine. The old Celts used the body of a crane to hold their tools because these tall, wading birds were said to embody secret knowledge. I have two of these bags—one stored in physical reality, and another kept in other dimensions, holding the less tangible tools I have been given.

Today, most "crane" bags are made of leather. To acquire hide for these bags, some suppliers hunt in the old way—with honor and dignity for the deer, cow, or elk. If you cannot find such a supplier, bless the hide that you do find and thank the animal for having provided it. Ask its spirit for blessings in return, as well as advice, since it may well become an ally. This animal spirit will be grateful for your love and help, especially if you go back to its death scene to ease its pain and shock. If you prefer a cloth bag, however, create or select one made of cotton, linen, hemp, wool, or other natural fiber.

The size and design of your bag are up to you. It should be large enough to hold your tools, yet compact enough to be easily carried. You could paint motifs on it or leave it unadorned.

*Cauldrons.* These are sacred bowls used for holding and seeing. Celtic shamans of old would fill their cauldrons with water and look into it for messages or visions, much as a present-day seer uses a crystal ball.

In essence, a cauldron symbolizes knowledge passed on as nourishment—a meaning brought to life in a sixth-century story titled "The Cauldron and Taliesen." Taliesen lived in Wales at the time and was chief bard of Britain. Although his poetry and songs live on today, his origins remain in the world of myth, as is revealed in the following abbreviated version of the story.

Ceridwen, a goddess skilled in magical arts, had two children—a son Morfran (Great Crow) and a daughter Creirwy (Dear One). Concerned about her son's ugly looks, Ceridwen decided to prepare a cauldron of wisdom and inspiration that would boil for a year and a day to make three drops of inspiration to help people honor her son for his wisdom and overlook his hideous appearance. Gwion Bach, a child of the village, was set to watch the cauldron as Ceridwen went to collect herbs. While she was gone, three drops sputtered out of the vessel and landed on Gwion's thumb, which he promptly licked to soothe the pain. In doing so, he derived all the knowledge there was to be had.

Immediately, Gwion fled, certain that Ceridwen would kill him when she found out what had happened. As she pursued him, he shape-shifted into a hare, a fish, a bird, and finally a grain of wheat, while Ceridwen herself transformed into various animals. Finally, she turned herself into a hen and ate the grain of wheat that was Gwion. The grain entered her womb, where it grew for nine months until a beautiful child was born. The child was so exquisite that Ceridwen could not kill him; instead, she placed him in a leather satchel and set him afloat on a river.

While fishing one day soon afterward, a nobleman came upon the satchel among a clump of reeds and cut it open. His first sight was of a "shining" brow, hence he named the child Taliesen (which means shining or radiant brow). So it was that Taliesen came to be raised as the son of a nobleman, and subsequently had many adventures as poet and bard.

Most cauldrons in Celtic practice are, like Ceridwen's, made of cast iron. For general use, however, bowls of wood or ceramic, or even large shells, are more portable and highly effective. It is best to avoid plastic and aluminum vessels, which give off residues. I use a fourteen-inch carved wooden bowl. For your own tool bag, choose a bowl *you* like and fill it with water during a full moon to draw in abundance. It can also be filled with water to reveal messages about your surroundings or to cleanse unwanted energy, which can then be cast into a river, or absorbed and neutralized by the earth.

***Talking staffs.*** Traditionally, Celtic shamans used four- to six-foot-long wooden staffs to gather information for clients. As shaman and client rested their hands on the talking staff, it would provide information about the client's life and offer suggestions on how to find balance.

To acquire a talking staff of your own, walk in the woods and look for a fallen tree limb that can be cut to just the right length. Or purchase a walking stick. In either case, know that your talking staff can aid you in journeying safely to other realms.

***The "Silver Branch."*** Referred to in many Celtic legends, the Silver Branch was seen as a connecting link between inner and outer worlds. Originally, King Cormac of Ireland received this branch from an "otherworld stranger" and used it to heal his people of physical ailments and imbalances. Many people today associate this branch with Cernunnos, the horned god of the forest, and also with the faerie people.

For a Silver Branch of your own, seek out a birch or alder branch. Then ask it what healing skills it has to offer you.

***Cloaks.*** In Celtic legends, cloaks often refer to a mantle of bird feathers called a *tuigen,* worn to signify a high level of authority. For the same reason, Hawaiian shamans of old wore capes of bird feathers. Donning such a cloak during ceremony, the wearer would move into another realm of being and take on the persona of the bird, a guide to information.

I came to appreciate the use of cloaks when one of my allies showed me the power of ritual dress and how it can serve as a tool for protection and transformation during ceremony. As a result, I now have a cloak on this side and one on the other that I use, when needed, for protection and invisibility. You, too, can wear a cloak for ceremonial "seeing" and "listening." Please remember never to use your cloak invasively or disrespectfully, for such an act may come back to you in the form of great difficulties.

Part Three

# Applying Ancient Wisdom
# in a Modern World

## Chapter Nine

# A Healthier Home or Office Environment

*Impossible only means you haven't found the solution yet.*
                                        —Unknown

Traditionally, balancing the energy flow through a building meant assessing the contours and energy lines of the surrounding land, evaluating the influence of the elements, and uncovering voids as well as areas of rushing, colliding, or stagnating energy within the structure. Today we must concern ourselves with much more, because as the life force passes through a contemporary setting, the building and its occupants are impacted by new factors—among them, a more mobile population, electrical voltage, and a vast array of toxic products.

Stability and environmental safety are therefore as important to practitioners of Gaiamancy as harmony, balance, and grace were to the old Taoists. A lack of groundedness, as we saw earlier, can draw us away from Gaia's protection and loving wisdom. Toxic settings, for their part, are physically and emotionally incapacitating. They also have a pronounced effect on *ch'i,* a matter that is rarely addressed.

Environmental illness (EI), also known as multiple chemical sensitivities, has been recognized as a disability by many federal agencies—

including the Department of Housing and Urban Development, the Social Security Administration, the National Institutes of Health, the Food and Drug Administration, the Environmental Protection Agency (EPA), and the Veterans Administration—as well as several corollary state agencies. When I first developed EI in the late 1970s, little information was available on alternative products and building materials, so I started researching on my own, talking to contractors and subcontractors, manufacturers, and other people in my predicament. Older artisans and builders told me how buildings were constructed before the chemical onslaught that followed World War II. In addition, I was able to locate a handful of responsible manufacturers committed to quality and safety. Among them, American Formulating Manufacturing (AFM) in San Diego, California, and Sinan Company in Davis, California, maintained a firm commitment to nontoxic and less-toxic products, as well as a willingness to answer questions. Theirs were the products I used in my own home and in specified commercial, residential, and government construction projects. Now, numerous manufacturers are following their pioneering lead in commodities ranging from cleaning products and shampoos to carpets and pet supplies. (For supplier addresses, see page 143.)

## Preventing Toxic Energy Attacks

Protection against environmental hazards is best achieved through education. Informed consumerism is essential, since the human endocrine system is profoundly sensitive and can be affected by even low levels of environmental exposures. Subjected to too much toxic overload, it can stop functioning, as I discovered firsthand.

To begin with, it is essential to study labels because, despite the increase in health-friendly manufacturers, some household and personal products are not what they appear to be. "Recycled," for instance, does not necessarily mean "safe"; it simply means that the materials were used previously and then turned into new products. The lovely white of many recycled paper products usually indicates that they contain traces of *dioxin,* a compound formed during the chlorine bleaching of wood pulp cellulose used in the original paper goods. Dioxin, considered the most toxic of all chemicals regulated by the EPA, causes cancer, birth defects, liver damage, skin diseases, immunotoxic effects, changes in endocrine regulation, and decreased vitamin storage. Other by-products of chlorine bleaching, such as *furans* and *chloroform,* are also highly toxic.

Chlorine itself, known to detrimentally affect ecosystems, has an intriguing history. This halogen element was used as a chemical weapon during World War I. Following the war, reserves of the gas, needing to be decommissioned, were poured into the manufacturing of household products. The more lucrative chlorine-based products proved to be, the more they were advertised, and the more obsessed Americans became with bleaching and disinfecting. By the end of World War I, chlorine had transformed from a weapon of war to the penultimate agent of cleanliness.

While studying labels to decrease the toxicity in your day-to-day environment, be sure to consider "bleach free" at least as important as "recycled." But remember, so much of our world is chlorine contaminated that you cannot avoid all exposures to this element. You might like soft toilet paper, for example, which most often is white. The solution, when faced with such dilemmas, is to follow your intuition and prioritize.

Examine labels on cleaning products as well. Choose perfume- and dye-free laundry detergents with the least amount of phosphorus and the fewest whitening agents. Twenty Mule Team Borax, for one, will remove odors and dirt while softening the water; it can also be used to repel ants and roaches. Get rid of those dryer sheets—although they may soften your clothes and fluff them up, they are filled with chemicals. For more tips on reducing risky chemical exposures, see the resource section at the back of this book.

In addition to studying product labels, begin to explore air quality. One common indoor air pollutant is *radon,* a colorless gas that enters the air through seepage from soil containing uranium and such materials as granite, shale, phosphate, or pitchblende. Radon has a smothering effect on *ch'i;* moreover, exposure to radon has been linked to lung cancer. To monitor for this pollutant, check the yellow pages for an EPA-certified testing company, or purchase a home testing device. Buildings in areas where granite is prevalent are often prone to radon contamination.

Other indoor air pollutants are composed primarily of volatile organic compounds (VOCs). *Formaldehyde,* one of the most damaging VOCs, is carcinogenic (cancer causing) and mutagenic (known to increase the rate of cellular mutation). This gas, also colorless, permeates buildings containing urea-formaldehyde foam insulation and resins—construction materials that were once banned. Symptoms of sensitivity to this toxin are asthma; ear, nose, and throat irritation; rashes; nosebleeds; depression; and damage to the central nervous system. *Ch'i* passing through formaldehyde can debilitate the will.

Other VOCs also show up in household products, as well as in such construction materials as paints, sealants, and adhesives. Many of these compounds can cause cancer, kidney or liver damage, and birth defects. Symptoms of contamination include eye and throat irritation. Although the toxic effects of some of these contaminants will abate over time, it is best to choose products that are free of VOCs.

How can you find out if a product contains VOCs? Ask the retail outlet for a manufacturer's safety data sheet on the product. If the retailer does not have one on hand, ask for it to be sent; manufacturers are required to furnish these sheets upon request. For more general information about indoor air pollutants or testing procedures, call the EPA at 800-438-4318. State agencies as well as your public health department are also prepared to provide you with information.

Plants can help save the day by absorbing toxins and purifying the air . . . up to a point. The National Aeronautics and Space Administration (NASA), while researching the safety of space stations, placed plants in sealed chambers filled with formaldehyde and other toxic gases. The plants reduced concentrations of the gases by up to 85 percent within a twenty-four-hour period. The results of this study reveal that the green people are indeed devoted allies: asparagus ferns and philodendrons are great benefactors; spider plants and golden pathos will absorb formaldehyde from furniture, fabrics, and cleaning products; daisies, lilies, and chrysanthemums will take up chemicals and VOCs from cleaning products, varnishes, and adhesives; and ivy will assimilate benzene, a toxic liquid used as a solvent.

Subjected to severe chemical overload or outgasing, however, our allies will die. One preventive tactic is to give plants a good airing from time to time, along with expressions of gratitude. Better yet, make wise consumer choices!

## An Environmental Assessment

Now let's go for a walk-through of your habitat. Here we will assess your home or office not so much in terms of placement and design—which you may have already tackled using the wheels of Gaiamancy—as with an eye toward unwanted environmental exposures. Turn-of-the-century quality of life hinges on the *totality* of these factors. As before, we will start with the outlying area.

### *Your Neighborhood*
Neighborhoods with long-term residents or commercial property owners impart stability and a hearty flow of *ch'i*. Why? Because people tend to stay where their lives feel full and abundant. But be careful not to judge stability as "good" and transience as "bad," because at certain seasons of life, transition is important for growth. If you are approaching one of these junctures, a neighborhood with a changing population and a variety of activities may be providing just the stimulation, support, and vitality you need.

If, on the other hand, your neighborhood has a high degree of transient energy and you are wanting stability, a number of stabilizing solutions are possible. One is to place objects or images that represent solidity at the heart, or center, of your home or work space. Grounding can be achieved by displaying pictures of peaceful settings, such as mountains—in which case smooth, worn facades and peaks are far better than sharp, craggy ones—or images of pyramids inscribed in metal or clay, but not glass, as it is too insubstantial for this purpose. If the heart of your site is a hallway or corridor, consider an oval or round area-rug in greens and browns, or think about installing a floor design in tile or wood. If you work in an office where "touch-ups" are prohibited, put out a firm, clear intention for stability, then reinforce it daily, mentally and in spirit.

Next, observe the street outside your front door. Is it winding or straight? Originally, roads conformed to the earth's natural contours; then in pre-Christian times, Romans introduced straight roads, because they allowed for easy troop and convoy movement. The grid system seen in today's major cities is a direct descendant of the straight lines imposed by the Romans, evidently with little understanding that winding roads contribute to human well-being.

The best way to counteract the rushing flow of *ch'i* resulting from the accelerated movement of traffic along a straight and level road is by keeping it *away from your door.* Wind chimes, wind socks, and other feng shui cures listed in chapter 8 can serve as effective safeguards.

To detect above- and below-ground energy lines, use dowsing rods or a pendulum. For less refined energies, such as direct or alternating currents around the building, invest in a gauss meter; these are available for between $40 and $200. The best detector of all, however, is your intuition. Pay attention to the "voice" of the land, which can be addressed through practice 8, and your body's reaction to it; your body will let you know where something is out of sync. The better you are at listening and feeling, the more likely you will be to intuit solutions geared to harmony and balance.

*Practice 8*

## Listening

This practice will help refine not only your listening but all your sensory perceptions. The more you work with it, the more quickly you will move into a receptive mode of being, until eventually it will occur instantaneously. (*Note:* Although the instructions that follow pertain to outdoor listening, this exercise can also be performed indoors to help you become more keenly aware of interior imbalances.)

~ Sit quietly outdoors. Close your eyes and take a few long, deep breaths.

~ Let your body relax, from your toes to the top of your head. When you are fully relaxed, you will be better able to tune into your internal communication centers.

~ With your mind and heart, ask to speak with the earth. As soon as you feel an open line of communication with Gaia, ask two or three clearly stated questions.

~ Listen for Gaia's answers. Listen deeply and patiently, as though you were engaged in a telephone conversation with someone you care about. If at any point you feel unsafe or uneasy, ask your guides or guardians for protection, although when you are truly tapping into the Source, your safety will not be threatened.

### The Land You Steward

Everyone stewards land, even penthouse dwellers. Why is this so? Because all buildings rest on a foundation that is held and supported by the earth.

To assess the land you steward, begin by sending your awareness into the earth, as described in practice 1 on page 15. Then pick up a handful of dirt and "feel" it. Placing a small amount on the tip of your tongue, as described in chapter 6, taste the "sweetness" of the dirt. (Make sure that the soil you are connecting with is free of chemical residues, petroleum by-products, pesticides, and other toxins.) What do your senses tell you about the health of the soil? If the land you steward is covered entirely by asphalt or concrete, then close your eyes and *intuit* the dirt beneath it. Remember, intuition is a powerful sensory organ.

After fully sensing the earth, call on the spirits of your plot of land. You will know they are responding by the images, smells, or messages you receive; you may also feel a tingling in your arms or legs, or chills down your spine. When you feel the spirits' presence, ask them about the balance and harmony in this portion of the earth, and using the sense of hearing you refined through practice 8 on page 123, listen for their reply. If you can't "hear" a response right away, try again later; because these subtle perceptions are not usually recognized in Western cultures, it can take time to tune into them. For best results, release all expectations, and treat yourself with understanding and compassion. In response to your patience, honoring, and respect, the spirits of the land will gift you with their wisdom.

In addition to gleaning information about the overall well-being of the land you steward, check for environmental toxins. A lawn treated with chemical fertilizers can pose numerous problems, in which case it is best to replace them with one of the many natural brands on the market. If you live or work in a condominium or an apartment, talk to the management or owners' association about switching to a less toxic product, and invite your neighbors' participation—there is more power in numbers! This solution alone will have a profound effect on your building's well-being and your own.

### *The Building You Live or Work In*

As we walk through your home or office, we will assess its level of toxicity. Because most building materials and home furnishings contain some toxicity, the key is to minimize its cumulative impact as much as possible.

**Front Door/Entry**

What faces your door? Ideally, the "mouth" of your building, like the mouth of your body, is taking in wholesome sustenance. Scanning the entryway, what do you see? If the front door is close to the street, you may need plants to absorb the carbon dioxide and other pollutants emitted by passing traffic. Good nourishment at the entryway is essential to a healthy, balanced living space.

With this in mind, you may want to get in the habit of taking off your shoes by the front door, so as not to track in lead and other toxins that can become airborne and ingested. If you enter the building through an attached garage, be sure to leave your shoes at *this* door. You may even want to place a basket of thick wool socks and a chair for shoe removal next to the front door, and tell friends and relatives that taking off their shoes is a courtesy to you and your setting. Although this practice may take some educating at first, especially in areas of the country where feet get cold, your guests will quickly feel at ease leaving the "outside world" at the door.

**Living Room/Lounge**

Do you have wall-to-wall carpeting? If so, there is a good chance it is outgasing VOCs, in which case you may want to seal both the carpet and the padding beneath it. (For companies that sell sealers, see the literature listed on pages 142 and 143.) Carpets also gather dust composed of mites, hair, pollen, and mold spores, as well as insect feces and parts. To eradicate these pollutants, purchase a good water-vacuum system and use it often. The best solution to carpet quandaries is regularly vacuumed wood floors with area rugs that can be shaken out.

Ductwork for heating and cooling systems should be cleaned on a regular basis, too. Check your yellow pages for companies that offer this service.

The living room or lounge is also a repository for electromagnetic energy emanating from appliances such as electric heaters, stereos, CD players, TVs, computers, and telephones with answering machines.

(Refrigerators, toasters, electric ovens, and microwave ovens can be just as problematic.) Electromagnetic energy disseminates positive ions and radiation, which over a period of time can interfere with intracellular communication, affecting reproductive organs, the pineal gland, natural bodily rhythms, resistance to cancer, and behavioral patterns.

Wires that run through living room or lounge walls are "hot" all the time unless you shut off the breakers at the electrical panel. In lieu of taking such drastic measures, you can lessen the likelihood of overexposure to positive ions by sitting at least six feet from the screen while watching television; at this distance the field output drops significantly. Also sit as far back as possible from your computer video display terminal, which emits ELFs (extremely low frequencies) loaded with positive ions. Negative ion generators can help neutralize this energy, although a simpler solution would be a fountain with moving water, which naturally diffuses negative ions.

## Kitchen

A kitchen can be a war zone of chemicals. Look under the sink, for example. What cleaning products are "in hiding" there? Ninety-five percent of Americans keep a brigade of toxic cleansers beneath the kitchen sink. Ironically, many families are careful to store these products out of the reach of young children, rarely stopping to think that the fumes should be kept out of the range of adults as well!

It is a good idea to replace toxic cleaning supplies with alternatives such as BonAmi cleanser, baking soda, and borax. White vinegar and tea tree oil serve a variety of purposes, from cleaning windows and cutting soap scum to fighting mold and helping clothes retain their color. Dishwasher soaps free of isopropyl alcohol are also available, as are drain cleaners that rely on enzymatic action rather than lye. In addition, replace aluminum pots and utensils with those made of stainless steel. Considerable research has linked traces of aluminum in the brain to Alzheimer's disease.

## Bedrooms

Most people spend one-third of their lives in the bedroom—all the more reason to ensure that these sanctuaries for relaxation and sleep remain as uncontaminated as possible. If you use an electric clock or clock-radio, move it away from the head of your bed, or better yet, replace it with a battery-operated clock. Use natural-fiber bedding, washing newly purchased sheets several times to remove the formaldehyde, and vacuum the mattress at least once a month. Vacuum under the bed more frequently to remove any "dust bunnies" causing respiratory difficulties or allergic reactions that impede sound sleep. If you use an area of the bedroom for storage, clear it out and clean it up. Here the key word is *de-clutter!*

One of my clients was so sensitive to the electromagnetic currents in her bedroom that she couldn't sleep at night. In addition to insomnia, she suffered from nervousness and dizziness. To address the problem, we decided to put a breaker for the electrical line at the entry switch in the bedroom so that she could turn it off before going to bed at night. This solution worked so well that as soon as the breaker was in use she began sleeping soundly and peacefully for the first time in years.

If you are having difficulty sleeping at night, before going to such extremes, consider using a simple gauss meter to read the ELF magnetic fields in and around your bedroom. Sources for these devices, as well as others that diffuse, reduce, or neutralize electromagnetic energy can be found in the literature listed on pages 142 and 143.

## Bathroom

If the kitchen turned out to be a war zone of chemicals, the bathroom may be a little arsenal of toxic cleansers, so check the cleaning products stowed under the counter. Replace those containing toxic chemicals with natural alternatives—and rest assured that the use of natural cleansers does not lead to tennis elbow! Seventh Generation's alternative toilet bowl cleaner works very well, and AFM offers a full line of cleaning products.

## Utility Room

With a watchful eye, clean out all toxic products from this area, and replace them with safer alternatives. In proceeding with this overhaul, you will be simultaneously reducing the risk of exposure to contamination and supporting companies committed to a safer home and planet. Regularly clean the lint tray in the dryer as well, to prevent these particles from entering the air you breathe. To minimize the likelihood of inhaling other airborne irritants, move appliances every couple of months, clearing out the dust and dirt gathered beneath them.

## Garage

If you have an attached garage, begin parking your car with its tailpipe pointing away from the building. Also replace as many volatile chemicals stored here as possible. Those you decide to save should be properly stored. Watch out for flammable materials such as rags, paper, and gasoline, keeping them safely stored as well. To discard containers filled with toxic chemicals, take them to the nearest disposal site. Most communities now have toxic-waste sites near or in conjunction with landfills.

## Backyard

Convert your backyard from a repository for fertilizers and other chemical-based products to a low-maintenance garden and play area. Check with a local nursery for endangered plants native to the area. Growing these varieties in your yard will eliminate the need for fertilizer, reduce your water usage, and be of great service to the land. If it is time to refurbish children's outdoor play equipment, look for nontoxic paints and stains. Swings, slides, and sandboxes made of lumber treated with arsenic can be replaced with equipment made of rot- and wet-resistant woods, such as cedar or Alaskan pine, or equipment made of metal.

## Chapter Ten

# Gaiamancy for the Yard and Garden

*Your house is your larger body. It grows in the sun*
*and sleeps in the stillness of the night and it is not dreamless.*
—Kahlil Gibran, *The Prophet*

Your yard and garden form the "outside rooms" of your living or work space. As such, they strongly influence the energy flow into the building. With an eye toward landscaping, you can arrange your yard and garden to correct exterior problems, or if none are evident, to simply honor the characteristic energies of the various areas. In addition to applying traditional solutions addressed here and in earlier chapters, be sure to take into account personal taste, geography, and culture as you create your own circle of harmony on your acreage, lot, city terrace, or tiny balcony.

To evaluate yard and garden topography, we will refer to figure 10–1, which shows a Northwestern yard plan overlaid with a Native American medicine wheel aligning south with the entry to the home. If you prefer to use the *bagua* or Celtic wheel as an overlay, or to align your yard plan with true north and south, please do so. In either case, begin your assessment by listening inwardly to the life force of the land. Then arrive at solutions to problem areas by working in partnership with the land spirits and other inhabitants of the site.

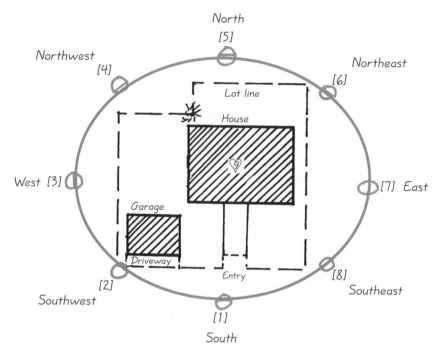

*Figure 10–1 Yard plan with medicine wheel overlay*

The house and garage in figure 10–1 are extremely linear. To soften the landscape, I suggested installing a curved path, rounded beds, and dome-shaped planting areas. Balancing the linear forces in this way evoked an instant feeling of synergy and friendliness.

## [1] South: Summer, fire

An area radiant with illumination, the south is often ideal for fruit trees, or even a kitchen garden celebrating the fullness of life. Be creative in the south, for creativity is the soul of fruitfulness. Also be sure to prune, trim, and weed any overgrown vegetation that obstructs the pathway and other flows of energy approaching the entry.

Because the entry to this home was bare of vegetation, I proposed a trellis with climbing vines of wisteria and honeysuckle to convey a sense of privacy. Defining a boundary between public and private areas sets a tone for transitioning from a social to a personal arena—an important preparatory task for anyone on the path of the warrior.

### [2] Southwest: Autumn equinox (September 21)
Here the wheel moves into the arena of personal growth and aspirations. Celebrate your growth in this area by painting symbols on garden stakes or on a garden wall. Because paints and other finishes used outdoors can leach into the groundwater and affect plants and animals, be sure to choose brands with the least amount of toxicity.

With the garage in the southwest, this yard called for plantings along either side of it and lining the drive as well. I recommended low-growing plants that would allow access to the house.

### [3] West: Autumn, water
In this place of emotions, consider a pond, birdbath, or fountain. Also pay special tribute here to the animal people that are part of your family or community. Animal people indigenous to the western portion of the medicine wheel are whale, dolphin, turtle, and bear.

Because this house is in the Northern Hemisphere, where the afternoon sun is intense, I recommended that the area be planted with vegetation that thrives on light. I also advocated for deciduous trees, to offer protection from the summer sun while allowing for an influx of light in winter.

### [4] Northwest: Winter solstice (December 21)
This is the place for moving into the stillness and listening. To foster introspection on this portion of your land, consider setting in place a bench, hammock, or stone seat.

Did you notice the void in this area in figure 10–1? To invite the missing piece of land back into the circle, I suggested the addition of plants or statuary. In addition, I advised the occupants to perform a welcoming ceremony by standing in the northwest, opening their arms wide, and with the aid of their guides and the land spirits, calling the missing piece to return home and make the energy whole.

If the void were repeated inside the house, correcting it would have required a very strong intention. With the area of introspection and nurturing darkness so chronically out of balance, the occupants would have had to consciously strive to incorporate these forces into their lives. Unattended to, such a void can lead to depression, disease, or serious family difficulties.

If your yard has a void in this area, one solution would be to plant a tree or sturdy shrub at the inside corner of the void. You could also place a statue of Kwan Yin here, to bring in warm, feminine nurturing. Or borrowing from the Native American tradition, you could set in place a solid round rock of deep red, dark gray, or black. While approaching such a rock, ask if it would be willing to hold the space; in response, you will receive an answer of yes or no. A fourth solution would be to complete the void with a prayer staff colored in white (representing north) and black (representing west). In such instances it is a good idea to install the pole so that its greater length stands tall above ground.

## [5] North: Winter, earth
North is often ideal for evergreens. If you live in the Southwest, consider desert piñons and junipers, which provide the energy of green year round and do well in varying degrees of sunlight. Since north is the place of the elders, it also lends itself to stones representing the ancestors. Ancient wisdom from around the planet could be set in place, defining a sitting area for retreat and sanctuary.

For this yard I recommended firs, to hold the energy of the north sweetly and strongly. Because firs also provide shelter and food to birds and squirrels, the occupants welcomed the suggestion as a "good neighbor act" toward their animal friends.

## [6] Northeast: Spring equinox (March 21)
This place of both stasis and moving into the fullness of growth calls for

celebration of the release from winter's hold, in the form of budding trees, animals awakening from hibernation, the song of frogs, and the return of birds. Bird feeders are desirable here, as are bulbs—daffodil, tulip, crocus, or lily of the valley—or if you live in a desert climate, Apache plume, purple aster, or yucca.

For this portion of the yard in figure 10–1, I recommended an arbor made up of flowering plants that thrive in cool, shady spots. Flowering vines are ideal for this area of awakening.

### [7] East: Spring, air

East symbolizes the waxing moon moving into fullness, and the yearning to be active. In warm climates, it is the place of seeding, perfect for berries as well as early-blooming plants, shrubs, and trees. In cooler climates, east is excellent for garden sculpture. Both landscaping options can provide inspiration on the path of the visionary.

This plot leaves little room for enhancement in the east, since the house sits so close to the lot line. I recommended airy plants such as deciduous shrubs to define the boundary.

### [8] Southeast: Summer solstice (June 21)

This is an excellent place for a butterfly garden composed of brightly colored flowers and plants. Annuals and perennials bursting with energy help celebrate the transitional nature of summer solstice, when the sun is at its fullness. If you enjoy dancing to the full moon, be sure to leave space in the southeast for dancing to the "full sun," the wildlife, and the long days of the season. This is just the spot for a sundial too.

To separate the yard from the street on this plot, I suggested a wildlife-supportive hedge of edible berries. In addition, I recommended tucking a compost pile in the corner, away from the front door and with easy access to the rest of the garden. Compost generates richness from waste, representing the processing one undergoes while moving into the time of harvest and bounty on the medicine wheel.

## [9] Center: Heart

The center, or heart, of a plot is best honored by stability. If the heart of your yard lies in the midst of flower beds or a row of shrubs, the land will be thankful. If instead your home or office holds some of the heart energy, acknowledge it with the sweetness of cultivated or wild roses, or any flowering plant that feels right to you.

On this plot of land, the heart is held by the pathway and the house. The pathway, however, allows for too much circulation and needs grounding. To ground the flow of energy here, I recommended curving the walkway and putting in strong, sturdy plants as well as rocks on the sides and in front of the house.

In the yard or garden, as in the home, the center holds special significance. It marks the place where all endeavors, desires, and momentum come around full circle to embark on the pathway to Spirit.

*Appendix A*

# Pronunciation Guide

## Chinese Terms

| | |
|---|---|
| Bagua | BA-kwa |
| Ch'i | ch'ee |
| *I Ching* | YEE-jing |
| Lo pan | LO-pan |
| Lung mei | lung-MY |
| Tao | dow |
| Ying lung | YIN-lun |

## Celtic Terms

| | |
|---|---|
| Ailim | a-L'EEM |
| Beach | BEE-ach |
| Beith | beet |
| Beltaine | BAL-teen |
| Bradan | BRAY-tan |
| Brän | braun |
| Brighid | bree-GEED or BREET |
| Cernunnos | ker-NU-nos |
| Cerridwen | ker-RID-wen |
| Coll | koll |
| Dagda | DOY-da |

| | |
|---|---|
| Dobhran | DO-ran |
| Duir | dur |
| Each | ech |
| Eilid | eeld |
| Faland | fa-LAN |
| Falias | fa-LAS |
| Fearn | farn |
| Finias | FEE-nas |
| Gearr | GY-arr |
| Gorias | GAR-us |
| Imbolc | im-BULK |
| Lug | loo |
| Lugnasadh | LOO-nas-ah |
| Luis | LOO-ees |
| Murias | MUIRE-as |
| Ogham | O-wam |
| Quert | kwert |
| Rön | RO-an |
| Ruis | roos |
| Saille | saul |
| Samhain | Sa-WAIM |
| Sidhe | shee |
| Taliesen | tal-e-ES-in |
| Tuatha Dé Danann | TOO-tha day do-NAN |
| Tuigen | too-GEEN |

*Appendix B*

# Glossary

*Ali'i.* Royalty of the Hawaiian islands.

*Bagua.* Divinatory oracle of the *I Ching,* based on a turtle shell.

**Cauldron.** Cast-iron kettle used for cooking and divining by early Celts.

**Celts.** Ancient peoples from Europe who migrated to the British Isles centuries ago. Some historians believe they were survivors of the lost continent of Atlantis.

*Ch'i.* Chinese word meaning cosmic breath, or universal life flow.

**Dowsing.** Method of divination originally employing a forked rod, often used to find water or minerals.

**Electromagnetic field.** An area marked by the presence of electrical currents flowing either above or below the earth's surface, or in the interior of a building.

**ELF (extremely low frequency).** A measure of electromagnetic radiation emitted by appliances that produce a magnetic field detrimental to physical, mental, and emotional health.

**Environmental illness (EI).** A contemporary diagnosis for a variety of symptoms arising from sustained exposure to toxicity; also known as *multiple chemical sensitivities.*

**Etheric body.** A sheath of energy that overlays and suffuses the physical bodies of all animate and inanimate beings; in Chinese medicine its currents are referred to as *ch'i*.

**Falias.** Northernmost of the four cities of the Tuatha Dé Danann; city gifted with a stone.

**Feng shui.** The Chinese art of placement.

**Fey.** Scottish for being naturally attuned; currently, slang for strange or odd.

**Finias.** Southernmost of the four cities of the Tuatha Dé Danann; city gifted with a sword.

**Gaia.** Goddess of the earth who, born from Chaos, gave birth without a mate to the sky, mountains, and sea; the living and breathing body of planet earth.

**Gaiamancy.** A compilation of spiritual and shamanic geomantic practices from around the world designed to enhance human and environmental health and well-being.

**Gauss meter.** A device for monitoring ELF 60Hz electromagnetic output, including measurements of levels above and below the recommended maximum ELF exposure of 2.0 milligauss.

**Geomancy.** Divination through geographic insights.

**Gorias.** Easternmost of the four cities of the Tuatha Dé Danann; city gifted with a spear.

**Intent.** Power of the human spirit to focus and project energy.

*Konji.* Characters in Chinese, Japanese, and Korean writing.

**Kwan Yin.** Chinese goddess of infinite compassion.

**Labyrinth.** A maze or spiral form often carved into the earth, representing a spiritual "journey" to a divine source.

**Ley lines.** Naturally occurring energy pathways found above and below the earth's surface, many of which were tampered with in ancient times; portions that remain have been identified as sacred sites.

*Lo pan.* A Chinese geomancer's circular compass used to assess correct siting for ordinary buildings, temples, and grave sites.

*Lung mei.* "Dragon lines," or currents of energy that run above and below the earth's surface.

**Medicine wheel.** A sacred symbol of the universal wheel of life "walked" by many First Nation peoples.

**Murias.** Westernmost of the four cities of the Tuatha Dé Danann; city gifted with a cauldron.

*Ogham.* A binary system of lines forming the ancient Celtic alphabet.

**Qi Gong.** A Chinese practice that teaches discipline, focus, and connection to *ch'i.*

**Shape-shifting.** The custom of taking on animate or inanimate forms through magic.

**Silver Branch.** A branch, usually birch, described in Celtic lore as invested with special powers and privileges from other realms, and usually gifted to wizards and shamans.

**Tai Chi.** A Chinese system of slow movements designed to teach discipline, focus, and connection to *ch'i.*

**Tao.** The guiding principle behind all reality, as conceived by Lao-tzu in the sixth century BCE.

**Totem.** A being, often an animal spirit, that serves as benefactor to an individual, family, or tribe.

**Tuatha Dé Danann.** An ancient race that inhabited the British Isles; children of the goddess Danu.

*Vastu shastra.* Vedic feng shui, originating in India.

# Resources

## Recommended Reading

### Chinese Practices

Collins, Terah Kathryn. *The Western Guide to Feng Shui.* Carlsbad, CA: Hay House, 1996.

Palmer, Martin, and Jay Ramsay. *I Ching: The Shamanic Oracle of Change.* Trans. by Zhao Xiaomin. San Francisco: Thorsons, 1995.

Rossbach, Sarah. *Interior Design with Feng Shui.* London, England: Penguin Books, 1987.

Waltera, Derek. *Feng Shui: The Chinese Art of Designing a Harmonious Environment.* New York: Simon & Schuster, 1988.

### Native American Practices

Arrien, Angeles, PhD. *The Fourfold Way.* San Francisco: Harper, 1993.

Bruchac, Joseph, and Jonathan London. *Thirteen Moons on a Turtle's Back.* Illus. by Thomas Locker. New York: Harper Collins, 1995.

Mails, Thomas E. *Fools Crow.* Tulsa, OK: Council Oak Books, 1991.

Mails, Thomas E. *Fools Crow, Wisdom and Power.* Tulsa, OK: Council Oak Books, 1991.

Wabun, Sun Bear, and Chrysalis Mulligan. *Dancing with the Wheel.* New York: Simon & Schuster, 1992.

### Celtic Practices

Conway, D. J. *By Oak, Ash & Thorn.* St. Paul, MN: Llewellyn Publications, 1996.

Matthews, Caitlin. *Singing the Soul Back Home.* Rockport, MA: Element Books, 1995.

Matthews, John. *The Celtic Shaman.* Rockport, MA: Element Books, 1991.

Thorsson, Edred. *The Book of Ogham.* St. Paul, MN: Llewellyn, 1992.

**Other Pathways**

Eliade, Mircea. *Shamanism: Archaic Techniques of Ecstasy.* Princeton, NJ: Princeton University Press, 1972.

Harner, Michael. *The Way of the Shaman.* San Francisco: Harper, 1980.

Ingerman, Sandra. *Soul Retrieval: Mending the Fragmented Self.* San Francisco: Harper, 1991.

Lee, Pali Jae, and Koko Willis. *Tales from the Night Rainbow.* Molokai, HI: Night Rainbow Publishing, 1990.

Linn, Denise. *Sacred Space.* New York: Ballantine Books, 1995.

## Environmental Books, Catalogs, and Newsletters

Baker, Paula, Erica Elliot, and John Banta, MD. *Prescriptions for a Healthy House.* Santa Fe, NM: Inword Press, 1996.

Bower, Lynn Marie. *The Healthy Household.* Bloomington, IN: The Healthy House Institute, 1996.

*Building Concerns Newsletter.* For architects, designers, contractors, and home owners. Available from Victoria Schomer, 415-389-8049.

Dadd, Deborah Lynn. *Nontoxic, Natural and Earthwise.* New York: St. Martin's Press, 1990.

*The Gaiamancy Catalog.* Available from White Doe Productions, 888-224-8652.

*Interior Alignment Catalog.* Available from Denise Linn Seminars, 206-528-2465.

Olkowski, William, Sheila Daar, and Helga Olkowski. *Common Sense Pest Control.* Newton, CT: Taunton Press, 1991.

Pearson, David. *Natural House Book*. New York: Simon & Schuster, 1989.

Pearson, David. *Natural House Catalog*. New York: Simon & Schuster, 1996.

Schomer, Victoria. *Interior Concerns Resource Guide*. For architects, designers, and contractors. Available by calling 415-389-8049.

*Seventh Generation Catalog*. Available by calling 1-800-456-1911.

Stein, Dan. *The Least Toxic Home Pest Control*. Eugene, OR: Hulogosi Communications, 1991.

Venolia, Carol. *Healing Environments*. Berkeley, CA: Celestial Arts, 1988.

## Suppliers

### American Formulating and Manufacturing (AFM)
350 West Ash Street, Suite 700
San Diego, CA 92101
619-239-0321

### The Feng Shui Warehouse
PO Box 6689
San Diego, CA 92106
800-399-1599

## Schools, Seminars, and Training Institutes

### Western School of Feng Shui
Practitioner training program
437 S. Hwy. 101, Suite 752
Solana Beach, CA 92075
Phone: 619-793-0945

### Denise Linn Seminars
### Interior Alignment
Professional certification course
Vision quests, trainings, seminars, consultations
PO Box 75657
Seattle, WA 98125-0657
Phone: 206-528-2465
Fax: 206-528-2469

### The EarthSong Center
Practitioner trainings in Gaiamancy
Classes, seminars, lectures, correspondence course
Feng shui, medicine wheel, Celtic wheel, shamanic practices
Maureen L. Belle, Director
PO Box AB
Greenbank, WA 98253
Phone: 888-224-8652
Fax: 360-678-3951

### Sacred Circles Institute
### Walking the Sacred Wheel
Teaching certification
Year-long initiation journey around the ancient wheel
Mattie Davis-Wolfe, RN, MA, and David Thomson, PhD, Directors
PO Box 733
Mulkiteo, WA 98275
Phone: 425-353-8815

# Index

# About the Author

Maureen L. Belle has a five-year degree in interior architecture and more than thirty years of experience in architecture and construction. A resident of Whidbey Island, Washington, she has practiced as a professional environmental consultant for the past ten years.

Growing up around construction sites as the daughter of a builder-developer, Maureen acquired an early interest in creating harmonious environments. Since designing her first housing tract at age nineteen, she has gone on to design and build homes and commercial structures in Arizona, California, Oregon, Washington, and Hawaii. She is currently director of The EarthSong Center, which offers trainings, classes, and apprenticeship programs in Gaiamancy, including an outreach program in cetacean-human conversation. This spiritual center is dedicated to healing the planet and her occupants.

# Order Form

| Quantity | Item | Amount |
|---|---|---|
| ____ | *Gaiamancy: Creating Harmonious Environments* ($17.00) | _____ |
| ____ | *The Gaiamancy Catalog* (no charge) | |
| | Sales tax of 7.9% for Washington residents | _____ |
| | Shipping and handling (see chart below) | _____ |
| | **Total amount enclosed** | _____ |

Quantity discounts available

**Shipping and handling**

| | Surface | First Class | Each Additional Book |
|---|---|---|---|
| United States | $3.50 | $.50 | $.25 |
| Canada | $5.00 | $1.00 | $.50 |

**Method of payment**

❐ Check or money order enclosed
(made payable to **White Doe Productions,** in US currency only)

❐ MasterCard          ❐ VISA

_____          _____

Card Number                                                    Expiration date

Signature  _____

Please photocopy this order form, fill it out, and mail it, together with your name, address, and personal check, money order, or charge-card information, to:

White Doe Productions
PO Box AB
Greenbank, WA 98253
888-224-8652